HOW TO
LEARN FASTER
AND BE MORE
PRODUCTIVE

Improve your Memory, Focus your Mind and Achieve Powerful Goals

Joseph Milano

Skill Builders

© Copyright 2021 - All rights reserved.

The content contained within this book may not be reproduced, duplicated or transmitted without direct written permission from the author or the publisher.

Under no circumstances will any blame or legal responsibility be held against the publisher, or author, for any damages, reparation, or monetary loss due to the information contained within this book, either directly or indirectly.

Legal Notice:
This book is copyright protected. It is only for personal use. You cannot amend, distribute, sell, use, quote or paraphrase any part, or the content within this book, without the consent of the author or publisher.

Disclaimer Notice:
Please note the information contained within this document is for educational and entertainment purposes only. All effort has been executed to present accurate, up to date, reliable, complete information. No warranties of any kind are declared or implied. Readers acknowledge that the author is not engaged in the rendering of legal, financial, medical or professional advice. The content within this book has been derived from various sources. Please consult a licensed professional before attempting any techniques outlined in this book.

By reading this document, the reader agrees that under no circumstances is the author responsible for any losses, direct or indirect, that are incurred as a result of the use of the information contained within this document, including, but not limited to, errors, omissions, or inaccuracies.

Your FREE Gift

This free bonus includes worksheets that have been designed to help you easily apply key lessons in this book.

Please scan the QR Code below and download.

CONTENTS

	Introduction	1
Chapter 1	The Keys to Your Success	7
Chapter 2	Building Your Memory Muscle	28
Chapter 3	Fall Down Seven Times, Get Up Eight	55
Chapter 4	Overcome the Beliefs That Limit Your Progress	75
Chapter 5	7 Steps to Faster Learning	83
Chapter 6	Next Level Note Taking	101
Chapter 7	Supercharge Your Mental Focus	112
Chapter 8	The Power of Consistent Action	126
	Conclusion	139
	References	145

Introduction

It's one of those hot Sunday mornings, and you decide to take a shower. As water pours down your body, and you are busy karaoke-ing a song in your head, something happens. A light bulb flickers above your head and draws a smile onto your face... You have an idea!

A thought emerged in your subconscious, and it felt like there was room for some information; the thought pushed into your conscious mind and revealed the solution you had been looking for the whole weekend.

The emergence of thought is the first step of conception for any idea to become a reality. It is one of the most amazing things that our mind is capable of producing. Every thought we have can be a ground-breaking idea, a suggestion to improve, or a goal we must set.

Everything we see, smell, taste, hear, or feel and then can recall the sight, taste, or smell of is because it is stored in the mind somewhere. Your favorite perfume, for instance. Or your grandma's shepherd's pie recipe.

It is all in the head. We just need to learn how to focus and bring it into the conscious. Each thought that we have creates neural pathways. More and more connections form when these neural pathways link to one another and form a memory. New research suggests that babies as little as two can recall an important event with precision. This further reveals the brilliance of the mind.

The reason our thoughts play an imperative role in our life is that they give birth to a certain mindset. Positive thoughts reap a positive mindset and a negative mindset yields a negative outlook. The right mindset empowers us to set the right goals, work attentively and with focus, and experience success in all walks of life.

The right mindset is the single most important factor in determining a person's success, professionally and personally. The thoughts we have consistently and directly impact our actions and behaviors. It is a lot like tracking metrics on social media. You click an ad or merely search for it on the internet, and then you start to see it everywhere. Once a thought enters the mind, it stays there for a purpose. Thus, getting the fundamental ingredient right is pivotal. The right mindset accounts for the basic distinction between those who succeed and those who don't. Once you become serious about achieving success, you must learn to master your thoughts and develop the right mindset. It is up to us how we connect the dots and create an effect that allows us to see the glass half full as opposed to half empty.

Our beliefs, biases, and attitudes affect how we process and interpret information. An optimistic mindset increases the chances of developing a positive and winning perspective. Tackling challenges, such as setting goals, increasing focus and productivity, and improving memory and learning abilities can become a lot easier if we begin with the right mindset. To successfully achieve any worthwhile feat, you must feel capable of accomplishing it, despite other things. Having an optimistic attitude increases your self-esteem too. It prepares you to build resilience and fight back against adversity. After all, self-dialogue can't be negative.

Other than that, the right mindset leads to the right drive and motivation needed to achieve any objective, big or small. Whether you plan to learn a new language, memorize a book, or head a global firm, you need the right drive and determination to begin. All these ventures will come with a set of unique challenges and obstacles that can only be tackled if you are strong-headed and motivated. You might be tempted to succumb to the difficulties because it seems like an easier way out but having the right willpower and state of mind will empower you to carry on fighting.

Believe me, reaching your goals requires more than a measly dose of motivation and desire. If you want something, you really must want it. You must be willing to go to all lengths to accomplish it. It begins with getting yourself in the right mindset of wanting it, mapping out how you are going to achieve it, gathering the right intellect and resources, and the right motivation and resilience to stay committed.

The same applies to when you are trying to take in more information and become a fast learner. Improving your memory is no different. It is a goal that you set. You want to memorize and have a better recall. You want to be able to lock in as much information as you can at a time without getting distracted. Improving memory is easy. We have all the information we need inside our heads. We just need to know how to unlock it. For example, if you were in an interview and the interviewer asked you to describe yourself and your achievements, you immediately begin to rearrange the memories in your mind, starting from your childhood achievements to college awards. You form an answer almost instantly. The memories in your mind are a representation of the life you have lived. You have been a data-gathering being from the minute you were born.

Think about it; imagine if you didn't have any memories. How would you remember things as simple as how to hold a fork or tie your laces? If you didn't have any memories, how would you have learned to communicate or excel in any task or chore? It is because of your ability to store information and then retrieve it the second you need it, that makes you who you are. Retrieval of memory is as important as the memory itself. Of what use will it be if you can't recall it for when you need it? For example, what good is remembering all the answers when you are out of the exam room, or what good is learning how to swim when you are in the depths of water, gasping for air?

Sadly, over the years, we have associated building one's memory with cramming rote memorization. We let students cram to pass exams without necessarily understanding the concepts or the material very well. Educators believe that understanding leads to recall. Try remembering all the jokes or poems you ever heard when you were young. You might only recall a few despite hearing hundreds of jokes and poems. But why does this happen and what are the ways that best help to commit things to your long-term memory without it being so hit and miss?

Remembering and understanding are two different things. We see and take in a ton of information about our surroundings and yet fail to recall when asked. Your mind is either too occupied to register this information or fails to recognize it. Understanding something only becomes useful when you practice what you have remembered to achieve instant recall.

But this isn't true for all types of learning. Reading, for instance, isn't something that originated in nature. It is man-made and therefore, it doesn't fall under instinctual skills. We have to learn to master it and hone it in our daily lives. This doesn't, in any way, suggest that we are incapable or incompetent to take it on.

With the right skills, learning tactics, and memory-building exercises and practices, we can all learn to absorb, retain, and recall information that we have been taught, have read, or viewed somewhere.

In this detailed guide on improving your learning skills and ultimately achieving enhanced productivity is backed by scientific evidence and includes excerpts from various pieces of amazing research on the subject matter. We will be looking at both old and new practices, techniques and exercises, along with their break downs and explanations that will help to bridge your barriers of learning, memory building and recall.

We will discuss the importance of mindset, strength of will and motivation because without all of these elements well trained and working in unison, any self-improvement task laid out before you can end up feeling near impossible.

If you have had trouble recalling basic information and have to go back to reading instruction manuals over and over again to get one seemingly simple thing right, this book is for you. It is also for those of you who find that after studying a particular subject, you can only recall some of the information you need while the rest of the required information seems either clouded or lost. It is also for those who struggle with learning and understanding new information because they have only been taught to cram. This book is for those who want to improve learning efficiency by getting the most out of every study session.

First things first, we will discuss how to set, plan and time frame your goals and how to give them power, which will play a be a major part in keeping your motivation levels high and ultimately pushing you to bring the big ideas that you have in your mind into the results that you have achieved in reality. This book talks about how one can attain the right mindset and improved focus by using simple daily exercises. You will look at how you can build and hone your memory to develop recall and how you can create learning action plans to stay motivated and avoid procrastination.

I am super passionate about this subject and am very excited to share with you the ideas that have helped so many of my clients. I hope that the information, exercises and advice in this book helps push you to the next level and gives you the results that you deserve!

So without further ado, let's get right into it.

Chapter 1
The Biggest Keys to Your Success
Are in the Goals That You Set

We, humans, are great planners, or at least we think ourselves to be. When asked where we see ourselves in the next five years, our answers are mind-blowing, to say the least. Some believe they will be vacationing in the Bahamas, while others are sure they will become the CEO of their firm. Some are more realistic and assume they will be in a better financial state than they are currently, while others plan to win the next American Idol.

As good as these goals are, they aren't necessarily realistic.

What we fail to realize is that without a clearly defined plan of action, goals are merely wishful dreams. To accomplish any goal, you must give your 100%, believe 100% and devote yourself to it with 100% commitment. Without a goal and proper planning on how to make it a reality, you may well end up sleepwalking through life without purpose.

If you don't know where you will be in the next five years, then you better start thinking and strategizing. On the flip side, if you're new to this and the thought of goals that are 5 years away feels like off putting crazy talk, perhaps start thinking about a quarterly goal (12 weeks) and build it up from there. Just like honing any skill, the more you set goals for yourself, the easier it becomes and less daunting long-term goals will feel.

Goal-setting is both an art and science. Goal setting lets us plan for the future and develop the fundamental skills needed to achieve it. It helps us in all facets of our life, be it our relationships, work, or well-being. Goals are the target at which we aim our proverbial arrow.

Research supports evidence that goal setting serves as a powerful motivator. As defined by Edwin A. Locke in his goal setting theory, employees are more motivated and perform with increased productivity when they have clear, actionable, and consistent goals. In 1968, he published his revolutionary theory in *Towards a Theory of Task Motivation and Incentive* (Locke, 1968). Locke proposed that when employees are given set goals, expectations, prompts, and consistent feedback, there remains no such thing as a challenge. He studied the power of goal setting rather than keeping general outcomes, given that the goals were both well-defined and measurable.

A few years later, Dr. Gary Latham reviewed and studied Locke's theory and confirmed the link between increased performance and goal setting. He also pointed out that the connection was both real and crucial. Later, they both collaborated and presented their publication titled, *A Theory* of *Goal Setting & Task Performance* (Tosi et al., 1991), which expanded on Locke's brainchild idea.

In the revised theory, researchers divided goals into two characteristics: intensity and content. The intensity was defined as the resources required to achieve a goal, whereas content was defined as the outcome of the goal. The theory emphasized that one must not look at only the outcome of a goal, but rather look at its journey and method too.

As defined by them both, the goal is the aim or object of an action. It often accompanies a specific standard of efficiency and time limit.

Is a Goal the Same as an Objective?

Having understood what a goal is, many people believe it is the same as having an objective. It is important to clarify that they both aren't the same and mustn't be used synonymously.

When we talk about goals, we often point at the bigger picture. They are abstract and set a wide and overreaching target for companies and brands to keep their eyes on. Think of them as the vision statement of companies. Goals determine the general ambitions and intentions, and they aren't always measurable. But, at least, goal setting is an imperative part of everything we do. It provides us with a basic path, if not the complete route.

For instance, your current goal could be to become a successful athlete or professional chess player. While it is good to have an aim, there aren't any specific actions or time frames that you have associated with that goal. You want it, but you still aren't sure as to how you are going to get there. Then, you also don't know what will happen once you achieve that goal. You don't know how it is going to affect your life. You also don't have any means to determine its success or failure. Everything is based on a hunch and a thought.

Goal setting helps individuals motivate themselves in pursuit of an achievement or a destination. Having lofty goals, whether in an organization or personal life, can create an environment that spurs actions.

Objectives, on the other hand, come after a goal has been set. Setting objectives is the next step that fosters a clear understanding of how to reach the desired destination. While goals can remain abstract and vague, objectives refer to precise and measurable actions and steps that you must take to move forward towards achieving your set goals. Objectives are usually time-bound and have specific targets.

To put it to practice, suppose your New Year's resolution was to lose weight. It is a goal that you have set for yourself. However, how you are going to lose weight, what practices you are going to adopt, what changes will you make to your diet, and how many hours in a day will you spend working out are all objectives that must be set to lose weight. Without set objectives, you will have little motivation to move forward with a goal because you lack the knowledge, resources, and methodology. If you set the goal to lose, say twenty pounds, there are several objectives you will have to set such as joining a gym, cutting back on sugar, refined and processed foods, improving sleeping patterns and drinking more water, etc.

Goal-Setting – The Basics and Benefits

The goal-setting theory is set on the premise that conscious goals affect action. It proposes that human behavior is regulated by consciousness and therefore, having action-oriented and realistic goals promote action. To put it simply, humans have the wisdom to determine what's best for them and set a goal to achieve them by instinct.

The goal-setting theory also looked at why some people performed tasks better than others. The theory discusses how motivation can speed the achievement of goals. Each individual must set personal goals and find the motivation to move in the right direction. Besides, despite similarities in intellect and skills, some people are still more efficient than others. The only differential is their level of motivation. Some are more driven and committed while others have to force themselves to perform. It takes common sense to conclude which individual performs better.

In another study (Schunk, 1985), lead researcher Dale H. Schunk studied how goal setting paved the way for success and positive emotions that accompany it. He believes that setting goals builds confidence in our abilities, and we perform better. He thinks goal setting encourages creativity and a thirst for new strategies. Finding improved ways to use our skills and push ourselves to research task-related knowledge not only builds self-efficacy but also promotes self-confidence.

According to this study (MacLeod et al., 2007); goal setting encourages better planning for the future. During the experimental study, participants that took part in a goal-setting intervention program showed significantly improved subjective well-being via better planning tactics than those that didn't take part in the program. As per the researchers, when we set realistic goals, we think with greater clarity and produce far better ideas. We set appropriate targets that facilitate the accomplishment of our goals. Our capacity to plan gives us some power to influence goal outcomes which improves our chances of success.

Researchers Paula J. Vincent, Pradeep Boddana, and Andrew K. MacLeod believe that setting goals improves our internal locus of control. During the studies, researchers looked at individuals with positive and negative outlooks towards life. They found that those with an external locus of control believed that positive and negative results are due to external influences, whereas those who had an internal locus of focus believed that their actions and skillset determines their success or failure. This allowed them to improvise their tactics and work harder to reach their desired goals. Those that blamed external factors for their success or failure showed a lack of goal-setting which led to their limited thinking and composure.

It is also believed that setting goals improves academic success. Students that enroll in four-year degree programs at university with a lack of clear goals and motivation didn't finish their studies. When offered goal-setting intervention programs, students showed a significant improvement in their academic performance (Morisano et al., 2010).

When appropriate goals are set, it becomes effective and crucial to success. Goals offer us the direction we need to focus our attention on a task. It enables us to adopt goal-relevant behaviors and prevent distractions and engagement in irrelevant tasks. For instance, if the ultimate goal is to improve focus, we must adopt behaviors, such as creating an action plan, setting a distraction-free space, turning off the phone, setting time constraints and disabling desktop notifications, etc. these behaviors can only be adopted when one has a clear goal in mind. In his book, *Organizational Behavior: Essential Theories of Motivation and Leadership*, author John B. Miner proposed three goal-setting propositions.

He believes that:

1. Goals invigorate performance via motivation to expend the required effort corresponding to the difficulty of the task.
2. Goals direct the attention of people towards relevant behaviors and drive them away from behaviors that are detrimental and irrelevant to the achievement of the task.
3. Goals motivate individuals to persist in tasks over time.

Goal-setting, as discussed previously, improves performance and productivity. Some other benefits of goal-setting include:

- Goal-setting is linked with higher self-efficacy. You feel more confident and empowered in your abilities and skills.
- Goals yield better performance and elicit a sense of satisfaction.
- Challenging goals result in outcomes valued by you. Meaning, when you overcome a difficult task or challenge, you feel positive and motivated to take on the next one. Not to mention, the level of satisfaction achieved is higher.
- Goal-setting keeps us going at a task for longer by improving our focus and concentration. It also prevents falling prey to distractions.

- When challenging goals are set, individuals require more attention and end up utilizing skills that remained unused previously.
- Goal-setting encourages you to seek better strategies and plans.

Locke and Latham devised five goal-setting principles that drastically improve our chances of success. These include clarity, challenge, commitment, feedback, and task complexity.

Clarity

Clarity refers to how clear and well-defined a goal is. Ideally, a goal shouldn't leave room for misunderstanding. Goals should be clear and explicit when it comes to what behaviors must be adopted and which ones will yield the most benefits. You should know what it will look like once the goal is achieved. The answer to this will help you set clear goals and objectives.

Challenge

A challenge motivates us. It encourages us to step out of our comfort zones and try something new. A goal shouldn't be too easy or boring. Or else, the satisfaction from achieving it will be minimal. It should be challenging enough to keep you on your toes and apply the best practices. But this doesn't mean the goal is unrealistic.

Commitment

To make a goal effective, it must be agreed upon first. Meaning, the goal should be in proportion to the established expectations. The efforts needed and the reward to be achieved must be agreed upon and clear.

Feedback

Feedback, especially prompt, can prevent you from going in the wrong direction. Feedback is possible when you track your goals and objectives. Meaning, you must know if your methods are in line with your end goal or not. If not, you must know how to rectify and start all over again to prevent failure. Feedback also provides you with a map of how far you have come from where you initially began. This can be uplifting.

Task Complexity

Continuing from the second point, when a goal is complex, it keeps one devoted and empowers them to think outside the box. However, you will be discouraged if you sense that the task is too complex or the time allotted to finish it is unrealistic. Therefore, ensure that you set realistic expectations when it comes to allocating each small task within a time frame. When tasks are too complicated, they can overwhelm a person and lead to procrastination.

How Goal-Setting Rewires the Brain

The power of goal-setting isn't anecdotal alone. As witnessed, there is a wealth of scientific research that goes into it. Here, I want to focus on how it changes the way the brain functions. This knowledge will help you set your goals more suitably and reap the most rewards.

According to an article published in Behavioral and Cognitive Neuroscience Reviews (Compton, 2003), goal-setting restructures the brain.

The amygdala is a part of the brain responsible for evaluating the degree to which a goal is important to you. The frontal lobe is the part of the brain that does most of the problem-solving and defines the specifics of the goal.

They both work together to maintain focus and develop motivation to drive forward. They promote actions, situations, and behaviors that make the goal accomplishable and prevent you from succumbing to behaviors and actions that distract you from your end goal or make it harder to achieve. This may sound simple, but it is more complex than you think. The brain can create new patterns and form new connections. This process is called neuroplasticity. A goal creates new ideas and thoughts. These thoughts further transform into behaviors and then actions. So to say that a goal changes the brain's structure when it is motivated to accomplish it is true.

This phenomenon was first studied during an experimental research study on patients with multiple sclerosis (MS) at the University of Texas (Stuifbergen et al., 2003). Multiple sclerosis is a type of degenerative brain disease with symptoms such as speech impairment, numbness, severe fatigue, and loss of muscular coordination. During the experiment, researchers divided the patients into two groups. One group was told to set ambitious wellness goals while the other group remained the control group. After assessing and monitoring their symptoms for some time, researchers found that those with ambitious wellness goals reported less severe symptoms than the other group. In short, goal-setting helped their brains fight the symptoms using neuroplasticity.

In another study (Cole et al., 2013), researchers aimed to determine what types of goals motivated the brain to rewire. Turns out, goals that are tied to some emotional aspect motivate individuals to seem less challenging than others. Meaning, if you have a strong desire to achieve something, your brain will make the obstacles seem a lot less daunting than they are. A similar expression is used to define when we fall in love, true love.

Setting ambitious goals leads to improved motivation. Easily-achievable goals aren't perceived as worthy by the brain, thus leading to poor motivation. When you are highly ambitious and the goal seems challenging, you develop a renewed sense of motivation and drive. In one study, it was found that when people set ambitious goals for themselves, they saved more energy than those that set an easier goal (Becker, 1978).

Simply put, if you want to activate your frontal lobe and amygdala to their full potential, then you must begin with setting ambitious and challenging goals.

Questions to Ask When Setting a Goal

Having understood what a goal is and what benefits it offers, the next logical question that crosses the mind is how to set one. For instance, if you want to know what goal is appropriate and necessary to set right now, you must evaluate your most important values presently. Knowing this will help you prioritize and identify your passions and desires. If you are focused on career advancement, you can identify what more you can do to improve your chances of winning a promotion. Could it be an advanced course, a training program, an internship, or new skill development, etc.? Once you have your options highlighted, you can prioritize based on which option offers the most rewards.

You must also ask yourself if your actions and behaviors align with your objectives. Continuing from the above example, you should map out how you are going to achieve the goal and assign yourself daily, weekly, and monthly tasks. The more engaged and focused you remain, the more devoted your mind will too. Another important thing to note here is that your actions must align with your objectives. For example, if you wish to get promoted, you might want to be on time daily and have all your work done and dusted before you leave.

As an ideal goal should be slightly challenging, the next question you must ask yourself is whether the set goal encourages you to step out of your comfort zone or not. Challenging goals have shown better success and satisfaction rates. They act as a bout of motivation needed to overcome it. It must promote creative thinking and enable you to improvise and problem-solve.

To set a challenging goal, ask yourself this: what are you afraid to try but always wanted to do? For example, you might have wanted to drop from an airplane and rely on yourself and your parachute while you glide through the skies and enjoy the serene landscapes. Or you might have wanted to try a new style of dancing or cooking or improve on your current skills. These are all examples of challenging goals that many of us are afraid to take on but deep down, we know they will be worth it.

Another hack to help you set the right goals is to ask yourself what you are most passionate about. It could be learning a new language, traveling, swimming with the sharks, reading, or gardening, etc. Finding your one true passion and following it is the key to living life to the fullest. You enjoy doing it, and before you know it, it doesn't look too challenging after all.

If you face difficulty pulling through or staying committed, go back to the reasons you came up with when you first set the goal. Ask yourself if you still feel the same zest and want it as bad as before or have you changed your mind? Sometimes, we act hastily when setting a goal, thinking this is what we want to do for the rest of our lives. However, as time passes, and we come to terms with the realities of the amount of work and dedication it requires, we start to fall behind on the objectives and lose sight of the end goal. This means time is wasted. Therefore, continue to assess your passion and devotion towards the goal you have set and see if you are still up for it.

Once you have set a goal, ask yourself if you have the space to make it happen and if not, how are you going to make space. It comes back to prioritization. If you are a grown man, providing for a family, you can't just quit a well-paying job to join a group of hippies and go town to town, surviving on cheap marijuana and pot. If you want to travel and relax, you can take some time off from work to pursue your dream. You can't quit your job when you have to pay the bills and leave your family unattended. Do you have the time and space in your life to pursue your desired goal at the moment? Do you have a lot happening in your life right now? You have to be honest with yourself about this. If you think that you don't have the time and energy to go after your goals, how will you achieve them?

Once you can answer that, next comes the question of your commitment to your goals. How much time are you willing to take out in a week to consistently stay on track of things and achieve your objectives? Consistency is a must. If the goal is to get in shape, you will have to work out every day without skipping in between. You can't skip a day and then work out twice the next day. You can't expect to reach your goal like this. You have to make time for it every day or every week, given what had been originally decided. For example, if given the choice between watching Netflix and working on your goal, you should always be up for the latter.

Finally, to track progress and stay motivated, repeatedly check in with yourself. One of the differences between those who accomplish their goals and those that do not is found in the individual's level of consistent commitment over time. Set yourself a scale of 1-10. Each day, ask yourself how committed you feel you have been to your goals that day. If you're totally focused and on target, your answer should always be a 9 or 10. It's important to be honest with yourself here. It's not about beating yourself up if you score low on a particular day. Honestly scoring yourself each day gives you a clear and concise insight of what improvements you need to make tomorrow that will keep you on your path of achievement.

Having a "Why"

I believe that the most powerful part to setting and achieving any tough goal is the emotional tie that you place upon it. The root of this emotional tie can be found by simply asking yourself the question 'why' you want to achieve the goal or in other words what makes it so important to you and how you will feel once you have reached it.

A goal itself is a logical target that you want to hit. The question 'why' uncovers the emotional reasoning behind it. Why do you want it so badly? Why do you want to make this change right now? To a lesser or greater extent, we are all emotional creatures and our emotions are so much more powerful than our logic. Don't get me wrong, setting a specific (logical) goal with trackable progress is extremely important because without that target, you would end up firing in the dark. That being said, the driving force behind what will keep you heading towards your goal, no matter how tough it gets and what will help you maintain focus on what you have to do, no matter what distractions lay before you, is found in the emotional tie.

Why, for the longest time, has been one of our favorite words. When we were young and had started speaking, it seemed like all our sentences began with a why. Why do I have to go to bed? Why does daddy have to go to work? Why is the sky blue? Why, why, why?

As parents, this question can feel like it's driving us mad! But we also know that this is how we learn and embrace new things. The questions we ask improve our understanding and promote learning. It can be a skill, a new language, or a new area of the field you have just joined in. Asking why adds to our understanding and awareness of all things. When we know the reason why we want to do something, we become more willing to do it. As stated above, linking emotions with logic will make doing the tasks that will move you forward seem almost easier. This is because it empowers the belief in your own abilities and if you believe in yourself, you will achieve for yourself.

When setting goals, this "why" results in more mental clarity, improved focus, and increased productivity. We feel a boost, more like a kick to do something. We don't have to rely on timers, reminders, or alarms to get us in a working mode; we are drawn to it naturally, with enthusiasm and excitement.

During one TEDx Talk by Simon Sinek, he stressed the essence of having a 'why' when setting goals and objectives in life. When asked where to look for that compelling reason to drive motivation, he told his audience to look within. Instead of telling others how something is done, tell them why you do it. Let them get the taste of the same passion that drives you. Having a strong why also expands your perspective. You can view things differently and assess them better. You can rise above the competition because no obstacle feels too great, and nothing has the power to stop your forward momentum.

A clear why statement almost always guarantees success because it makes you stick by your values, truths, beliefs, and instincts no matter what. The 'why' serves as an emotional compass that no matter where you stand, will always point towards your desired destination. It gives you a purpose for the actions that you need to implement to get you to where you want to be.

Having a 'why' builds focus. It improves concentration and motivates you to stick to your goals. It helps you pave new ways to think differently and develop methods of doing the things that will move you forward.

As an example, take meeting a potential client for a presentation. You know that signing them up will take you a step closer to achieving your goal of marketing your brand globally. You ensure that all will go well, from the presentation to the meeting. You make sure that the room is clean, ready, audiovisual technology is working fine, refreshments are set, the projector is running, and the presentation has been run through several times to ensure it doesn't stop working mid-way, etc. But why make all these checks before the meeting? Simple, because by making all these checks before hand, you massively increase your chances of landing the client. This is an example of how by placing an emotional tie upon your goal makes running through the tasks to achieve said goal not only seem easy, but obvious.

No matter how insurmountable your goal may seem, putting some emotional weight behind it will make you find a way through. Whatever motivates you to give your 100% is your why.

When you have a strong reason, you don't fall prey to distractions and nuisances either. It helps you find your true passion and go after it. It gives you hope and direction. It gives you the mental clarity you need to become unstoppable. A 'why' will shape your life for the good. It will give you a purpose to go after, a wish to fulfill, and a dream to live for.

Having a 'why' when setting a goal, also brings a flow to your consciousness. You allow things to happen without fighting back. You change because you must. You adapt because it makes you a competent being. In short, you build resilience, embrace change, and find the confidence to move forward with a goal.

Setting Daily and Weekly Goals – Your Cheat Sheet

Lack of goal-setting causes disorganization. It leads to a purposeless life. We all set goals for various aspects but the biggest reason we fail to achieve them is that we don't know how to. We don't know how to proceed, track, or measure progress. The first challenge that comes across makes us want to surrender because we aren't motivated enough, to begin with. Although writing a goal is important, you must find ways to ensure that you achieve those goals within the time limit set by having objectives and tasks.

Depending on how big or small the goal is, you can create daily, weekly, monthly, or yearly goals by dividing the end goal into smaller ones. You can create a list of all the objectives and prioritize them based on their importance and urgency. You can even allot each goal a scheduled time to ensure it gets done. It is rather simple. Here's how you can begin setting daily and weekly goals.

Start with an abstract goal in mind. It can be as big as the skies. You can always break it down and assign tasks to achieve on a daily or weekly basis.

You can achieve a lot more than you probably realize. That's why the goal that you set should push you. This push will lead to you performing at a much higher level. This in turn will put you into a high achieving mental state where the path becomes crystal clear and almost anything is possible. Pushing yourself and elevating your mental state plays a big part in fueling your ability to bypass the mediocre and achieve truly outstanding results. It's better to aim high and miss than aim low and hit, or worse, still miss.

Once you have your goal in mind, begin getting down to the specifics. Brainstorm the ideas, behaviors, and actions you will need to perform to achieve it. This will give you a clearer picture of what to expect. For instance, if you plan to study for your exams, your goal shouldn't be just to "study every day." Instead try to think in terms of, how many days in total do you have to revise? How much time you will be dedicating each of those days and to which subjects? How many chapters of which reference books will you cover on those specific days, etc?

Similarly, if the goal is to start your blog, know how much time you will be able to set aside to create original content to posts each day? What topics will you be writing and posting about each day, week, or month? How much time will go into your research? Who will edit, format, and publish it, etc? Get down to all these details when creating daily, weekly and monthly action plans.

Be honest with yourself about the time frames you need to achieve a desired results at the quality level you're happy with. You should allow yourself enough time to complete each short-term goal before moving on to the next, always leaving yourself a little bit of room to reflect in between tasks so that you don't become overwhelmed. If the time that you set yourself to fully complete a task is too short you are likely to end up off target. This can lead to you becoming demotivated, and demotivation often leads to procrastination. If this does happen to you, don't fret. While you reflect between tasks, take back control by adjusting your time frames enough to make them realistic before continuing.

Set benchmarks for each day. Set deadlines so that you can track your progress and not lose sight of the end goal. When you finish a task before a deadline, not only will it give you some free time to enjoy, but it will also increase your motivation.

To properly track your progress, use a calendar, a memo, or an action planner app on your phone. This will remind you of how far you've come as well as let you know how much work is left before you reach your goal.

Use time-blocking to get on with your goals for each day. Time-blocking simply involves assigning blocks of predetermined time to different the tasks categories that you are aiming to complete. When each day comes scheduled this way, getting on with the focused work required to fulfil each task (both goal related or otherwise), rather than just winging it without a schedule, will make moving forward with your goals feel so much easier, leaving you less likely to become frustrating or to take away family time. Following a simple plan like this works like a check list and feels extremely satisfying each time a scheduled task is complete and essentially, checked off. For example, you can assign an hour to finish off daily chores, then assign an hour to exercise, another to get groceries, and then a few hours (or as many required) to work on your daily goal related tasks.

Schedule an end-of-week ritual to go through your progress and reflect on your goals. This way, if something from hasn't been completed in full it can be rescheduled, if something can be perfected, you can allow another hour to revise and format, if some methods need to change, you can do so too.

Finally, know that the best time to start working on your new goals immediately after setting them. As this is when your motivation will be at its highest, you will experience heightened mental clarity and your plan of action will be clearest in your mind.

The keys to success are found in the goals that you set.

Summary

▸▸ Set specific and measurable goals.

▸▸ Always set a time frame.

▸▸ Get uncomfortable! Make sure that your goal pushes you out of your comfort zone so that your subconscious mind sees it as worthy of your time.

▸▸ Ask yourself 'why?'; Why do you want to achieve the goal? Why is it important to you? Remember that emotion is so much more powerful than logic which is why an emotional tie to your goal brings with it clarity, drive and power.

▸▸ Set yourself daily and weekly goals. A simple schedule of tasks acts like a map that leads to your goals.

▸▸ Be honest with yourself. At the end of each day, score your performance from 1 to 10. Did you complete everything on your daily schedule? Are you now closer to your goals than you were this morning? Remember, your score should always be 9 or 10!

▸▸ Get on it! The best time to start working on your goals is now!

Download your goal setting and daily score materials from:
bit.ly/howtolearnfasterbook

Chapter 2
Building Your Memory Muscle

From the minute we are born, our brains are bombarded with a vast amount of information about who we are and the world around us. So, in our little brains, we try to store everything that we can and learn as we grow. This information takes the form of our memory when we store it inside our heads. Humans have the ability to retain different forms of memories for different periods of time. Short-term memories are forgotten after seconds whereas long-term memories stay with us forever. Our brain has a working memory that allows us to store information in our mind by repeating it for a limited time. For example, you can remember and recall a phone number if you keep repeating it. This is your working memory at play.

Another way science categorizes memory is by the subject itself, whether you are aware of it or not. Explicit or declarative memory comprises all the memories you experience consciously. The majority of these are common knowledge like the capital of a country, the color of an apple, or odd numbers from one to ten.

Implicit or non-declarative memory builds up unconsciously. Procedural memories are the most common among these. In procedural memories, the body remembers what you have learned or experienced. Riding a bicycle is one of the most common examples. Playing an instrument, speaking a language fluently, or remembering the names of your parents, siblings, and friends are also examples of implicit memories. Non-declarative memories are as important as declarative memories as they shape our body's natural and unthinking responses. This is the reason why you get tensed up when afraid, tear up when sad, and salivate when presented with your favorite dish.

Explicit memories are easier to form than implicit memories. You will require less time to learn the name of a country's capital than to learn to play an instrument. But, non-declarative memories (implicit) stick around. You are more likely to remember how to play a song that you learned on an instrument years ago and forget the capital of a country you heard about last month.

If all of this sounds interesting, there's more to come. In this chapter, we dive right into the science of how memory works, how it is formed and how we recall and retrieve memories. We will also look at how to build your memory like a muscle with some interesting exercises and simple techniques to improve recall and retrieval.

How Memory Works

To describe memory, think of it as an ongoing process of data retention over time. Learning about it and knowing how it works is crucial to understanding how we make sense of the world and take action. In the light of research, we know that memory operates via a dual process. System 1 consisting of the unconscious, routine thought processes interacts with system 2, consisting of conscious, more problem-based thought processes. These two levels, in turn, have processes that we receive information from, store it, and then get it back out when needed. Understanding the basics of how these processes come into play and make memories can help us in learning and controlling how much information we allow to be introduced, how to categorize it, and when to use it. This aids in the building of, what we call, creative or critical thinking.

To further elaborate on the dual-process theory, try to recall an incident or time when you experienced something memorable or learned a new skill, like driving a car. When you first learned to drive a car, every action was the result of a calculated plan. You were acutely aware of what was going on and what your actions were making the car do. You had to pay attention to every movement you made whilst staying vigilant on the road. During this analytical process, you were also aware of the reason why you were doing what you were doing. You knew that each step worked together as a comprehensive whole.

As your ability to drive a car improved, performing the skill required less cognitive thinking and driving became more intuitive. In other words, instead of breaking down each element that will make the car smoothly pull out of your parking spot and drive forwards after checking it's safe to do so you simply think, look and go. As your driving ability improved further, you were able to perform other intellectually demanding tasks such as creating a mental list of the groceries, listening to music, or looking for solutions to a problem in your head at the same time as you are able to safely drive.

This is the simplest way to break down the dual-process theory. The term dual-process determines that some behaviors such as decision-making involve systems 1 and 2 collectively. Where system 1 is characterized by unconscious and automatic thought, system 2 is characterized by intentional, effortful, and analytical thought. System 1 is linked with recall and memorization of information and system 2 is linked with critical or analytical thinking.

Moving forward, the three processes that both of these systems perform include encoding, storage, and retrieval. A basic knowledge of these will help us understand the working of memory better.

Encoding

The process through which we get information in our brains is called encoding. It is the input of data into the memory system. After receiving sensory information from our external environment, the brain codes or labels it. Labeling means the brain tries to associate it with the other information present previously and pieces it together. The process of encoding occurs through both system 1 and 2.

In simple terms encoding can be broken down into three types: semantic, visual, and acoustic. *Semantic encoding* involves the decoding of words and their meanings. The process was first demonstrated by William Bousfield in an experiment where he asked a group of participants to memorize a list of words. Each of the participants were given sixty words that were divided into four categories. The participants, however, weren't made aware of the categories and were presented with the sixty words in a random order. When they were asked to remember the words, they mostly recall them grouped into their corresponding categories. This meant that not only did they remember the words, they also paid attention to their meanings as they initially reviewed them.

As an example, suppose I give you ten words.

1. Car
2. Apple
3. Tomato sauce
4. Train engine
5. Insect
6. Towel
7. Bus
8. Vegetable
9. Cockroaches
10. Mattress

Now, you have five seconds to memorize them before I ask you to recall them. You are most likely to group the words train engine, car, and bus together because they all belong to the same category, means of transportation. Similarly, when recalling, you will link words like apple, tomato sauce, and vegetable together because they belong to the category of eatables.

Visual encoding, the second type of encoding, involves encrypting images. In visual encoding, we form images in our minds when we hear a word. For example, if I were to ask you to tell me who your best friend is, you will instantly reply with a name and in your mind, an image will appear too. It will be the image of your best friend or a memory that you cherish. Similarly, if I tell you to read the following words: car, apple, bus, wisdom, honesty, value, and then ask you to recall them a minute later, you are more likely to remember the first three (car, apple, and bus) than wisdom, truth, or value because you can associate a mental image of the first three in your mind. The car, apple, and bus created an image in your mind, and it got stored in your memory. However, the last three words had no definite image associated with them and therefore, you are less likely to be able to recall them as easily later.

The third is *acoustic encoding*, which involves playing along to sounds you once heard. For example, imagine you are in your car and on the radio, a song comes on that you used to listen to when you were younger. Surprisingly, you know the lyrics by heart and can recall every word as the song plays through. The same applies to tunes. We can instantly recall the 'happy birthday' song when it is played on a piano, violin, or flute. The reason we can do so is that our brain remembers the sound each word makes rather than just the words themselves.

Storage

For any memory or information to stick and be committed to long-term memory, it will first pass through three stages: sensory memory, short-term memory, and long-term memory. These three stages were first discovered by Richard Atkinson and Richard Shiffrin in 1968. They believed that humans processed information the same way a computer does. They called their model the Atkinson-Shiffrin (A-S) model.

Sensory Memory

According to the (A-S) model, stimuli from the external environment get processed first in sensory memory. Here, storage of brief events takes place like sights, tastes, and sounds. They last only a couple of seconds. Our mind continuously bombarded with sensory information. Even right now, as you are reading this, your mind is taking in and filtering more information than what's written here. The reason we filter most of this extra information out is because the brain is unable to absorb and store it. If this filter was switched off even for a moment, the flood of information about any random thing unrelated to what you are currently concentrating on would make it impossible to focus. For example, can you recall the color of your boss's tie that they wore last Monday, or what the number plate of the last cab you took was? Unless the tie had a distinct print that you either specifically noticed or commented on and the cab's number plate reminded you of something relevant to you, such as an important date, you are less likely to recall it. The brain discards any sound, sight, smell, or texture that it doesn't register as important or necessary. Only things that we view as valuable are pushed forward into the short-term memory.

Short-Term Memory

Short-term memory is a temporary storage unit that stores incoming sensory memory, also referred to as the working memory. After the information from the sensory memory is pushed forth to the short-term memory, the brain tries to connect it with something that is already stored in the long-term memory. This storage lasts for about twenty seconds. You can picture it as a photograph or document in front of you. It is up to you to either put it in the photo album/save it on the hard drive or discard it.

Long-term Memory

Long-term memory is where all the valuable information goes to get stored. It is a permanent storage unit without any time limits. What enters the long-term memory isn't forgotten under normal circumstances. It records and can recall all memory data that was stored minutes, hours, days, weeks, or years ago. If we continue with the computer analogy, think of it as the document you saved on the hard drive. It may not always be in front of you on the desktop home screen, but whenever you need it, you can open the folder and click on the file to retrieve it. Sometimes, long-term memories, that are seemingly buried deep in your mind aren't quite as easily recalled. In this case, usually a simple related prompt will 'jog the memory' and shift it back into the front of your mind.

Retrieval

Finally, the process of retrieval or recall is the act of remembering or bringing information from memory storage to conscious awareness. This is a lot like opening a document you saved on your desktop before. It is now in front of you after being stored on the computer's hard drive. The process of retrieval is important for our survival because it allows us to get through daily tasks while constantly improving on previously learned skills and knowledge so that we can perform at our best.

The Complex Process of Recall

In a memory recall, there is a replaying of neural activity that originated in the brain previously during a specific event. If another similar incidence occurs, the brain associates it with the original memory. This allows it to remember the details of that event and bring it into our consciousness. I used the example earlier that memory recall is kind of like pulling files from a computer hard drive, but if you look deeper, it is a rather creative and interesting process. The brain, among the trillions of thoughts and memories, finds that one stored piece that relates to the new information that is being presented. It's mind-blowing to see how quick and accurate the brain can be.

There are several main types of memory recall that that will be worth our time looking into. Let's review them one by one to gain a better understanding before moving on.

Free Recall

During free recall, you can remember a list of items in any order. Two different types of effects can be seen in free recall–primary effects and recency effects. Here are examples of these free recall types in action; with primary effects, you can recall items on a list that was presented at the beginning of the list or if they were presented multiple times on the list. In recency effect, you can recall items that were presented last on the list or the items on the list that you most recently read through.

Serial Recall

For ease of explanation here, let's stick to the same example as we used above of running through a list of items. Serial recall involves the remembering of items on a list in the order they were presented. In other words, one item on the list becomes a memory cue for the next item on the list. Serial recall is how we are able to remember our life's events in chronological order.

Interference with Memory Retrieval

Interference in memory occurs where there seems to be an interaction between new and previously learned materials. Interference in memory can either be proactive or retroactive. Proactive interference refers to the forgetfulness of new information due to interference caused by previously learned knowledge that has been retained in the long-term memory. Sometimes these stored memories inhibit the processing of new memories. This happens most commonly when the new information is similar, in terms of context, but is not the same as the information that has been previously learned and stored. This is one of the reasons that when you get a new cell phone number, at first you have a hard time remembering it, and even though you know that it's now different from before, the old number remains stuck in your head.

Retroactive interference happens when some new information interferes with the encoding of previously learned information. For example, if you were asked to recall an event from your past and then immediately presented with some new piece of information, interference occurs where your brain has a difficult time recalling the initial event because it is busy registering the new information. Sticking to cell phones as an example; if you were given a cell phone from the early 2000s, even though it would be extremely basic by today's standards, you would be quite likely to have a hard time using it at first because you are so used to using the latest design.

Cued Recall

Cued recalls rely on a list of cues and guides to recall a memory. In cued recall, you can retrieve stored information that you weren't able to with free recall. Cues help the mind create new connections with an old memory, thus aiding in its retrieval. You may even be able to recall something you had practically no way of remembering without the prompt. For example, you might remember having a big birthday party when you were three years old only after you were shown a picture in a photo album that showed you with your favorite gift of the day in hand. You may not recall all the bits and pieces but you will be able to create a good mental image with what you can remember about that day. The stronger the cues, the faster, more accurate and greater volume of stored memories will be retrievable.

How Are Memories Retrieved

To retrieve a memory, the brain must revisit the neural pathways formed during the process of encoding and storage. There are different opinions on how long it takes for a memory to be retrieved, but it is safe to say that it depends on how strong the neural connections were formed during encoding. There is still more insight and research required to understand the exact mechanism. For now, science tells us that we can only retrieve short-term and long-term memory. There are different forms or patterns of memory retrieval that facilitate us to understand it better. These include:

Recall

Recall is the power to remember something without it being physically present. Recall refers to pulling information from the brain, for example, recalling somebody's name without hesitance or answering some basic yes/no questions. When you recall something, neurons in the memory become activated and reconstruct the memory at lightning speed.

Recognition

Recognition requires some form of cue to identify a thing. It can be an object, name, place, or thing. For instance, you may recall someone's name by seeing a photo of them in a photo album. Or when you can't recall the name of the place that you're traveling to but then remember it the moment that you get there.

Recollection

Recollection involves rebuilding or piecing together a memory. Here, the mind uses logical cues and structures to reconstruct the memory. For instance, you may recall the details of a particular night out once you receive some partial cues to the events that took place on that night.

Relearning

Finally, relearning refers to repeated learning of something that you previously studied but can't quite recall. Relearning greatly improves your ability to store and retrieve information. The more you relearn, the stronger the neuronal connections will be, further aiding in the quick recall. It's almost like doing more sets and repetitions of an exercise in the gym to improve your muscle strength.

The process of relearning (revisiting previously studied information) in short will present the cues that will in turn bring the previously learn information flooding back. This is a prime example of why having the ability to take super effective notes, especially when learning new specific information (such as when in a lecture, at a seminar or in a business meeting) is an extremely valuable skill. Reviewing information from a set of well-structured notes, can massively speed up the process of relearning many hours of information in a matter of minutes. We'll discuss various effective methods in a later chapter.

Can We Build Memory Like We Build Muscles?

Many studies suggest that our brains have incredible adaptability. We can train it to improve cognitive functioning, thanks to neuroplasticity. In neuroplasticity, the brain creates new neural pathways as well as makes connections stronger with every repeated action until they become a part of us (a habit). Brushing your teeth first thing in the morning is an example of this. Through constant and consistent repetition, the act has become so strongly ingrained that it has become almost automatic.

Speaking of training the brain, scientists today believe that the power of the mind can be trained following similar principles to building strength and endurance in a muscle. When you train at the gym, you are forcing your body to adapt to the overloads that you place upon it, which is why you become stronger, faster, increase your endurance, and improve your flexibility. Then while you recover (especially when you're sleeping) your muscles develop. Therefore, the more regimented your training schedule is and if you diligently stick to your nutrition plan, the faster and greater your results will come. Although the brain isn't a muscle in the same sense that your bicep is, it can be trained with a similar set of rules.

As a side note, I'm probably going to drive you crazy with the number of times I talk about consistency, but without constant action towards your goals (whatever your goals may be) you're very likely to end up disappointed!

Just to be clear, I realize that the brain, is a far more complex structure than that of a muscle. It doesn't contract or relax like a muscle. It stays supported in one place via a constant supply of fluid. So, in short, when I compare building the brain to building a muscle, I am referring to the fact that by placing an appropriate information overload onto your mind and repeating this process consistently over time, the brain gets an excellent workout schedule which can build up the endurance of focus and can promote memory gains.

Multiple studies propose that by stimulating the brain as mentioned above, we can improve all cognitive functions and massively reduce or even totally prevent cognitive decline.

So basically, the brain adapts and responds to mental stimulation in the same way that the body adapts and responds to a hardcore workout session. The more you focus your mind in a structured and thought-out manner, the more trained it becomes.

The human body is a powerful machine and must be taken care of to ensure its optimum performance. By keeping a healthy body via regular exercise, a healthy diet and enough sleep, the brain will be in a better position to perform at its absolute best. It is still possible to have some noticeable improvements in your focus and your memory without taking this into consideration, but always remember that the benefits you will receive are always comparable to the total effort that you put in.

Healthy Body + Healthy Diet +
Consistent Action = A High Performing Brain

How New Information Is Learned and Stored

No one has a fixed IQ. Science believes that brain development and intelligence are plastic. When stimulated, they expand. Environmental stimuli constantly alter the function and structure of neurons and the connections they form. This means anyone can build their brain beyond what they thought or believed.

Not long ago, there was an assumption that said that brain cells stop growing after we turn twenty. Only recently, through the discovery of neuroplasticity, we know those interneuron connections continue to be constructed and pruned in response to experiences and learning throughout our lives.

When an encoded short-term memory is developed, it must still be activated several times and respond to a variety of prompts to enhance its durability. Each time, we encode a new piece of information, a number of neurons get activated. If the memory is not repeated or activated immediately, it can easily be lost. However, if the action or pattern is repeated, especially straight after it has been learned, the same neurons respond again. The more frequently an action is repeated, the more dendrites interconnect and grow. This results in greater memory storage and an improved recall ability.

Practice makes progress – doesn't just sound like an idea now, does it?

Here's an example of this in action in simple but relatable terms. You're a party and make a new acquaintance, then almost immediately forget their name! How can you commit their name to your memory in the first few seconds of meeting them and avoid the embarrassment of asking for their name again? Simple, when you introduce yourself to them, make sure that you include their name in what you say, e.g. "Nice to meet you David. I'm Joseph"

Furthermore, retention can also be promoted when new memories connect with other stored memories due to their commonalities or differences. If we use visuals and graphic organizational tools, we can derive more connections and promote memory storage in different parts of the brain like the prefrontal cortex.

A good example of this is to imagine that you are taking an advanced course in college. Each class you attend takes the basic information that you have learned and applies it in increasingly advanced settings. However, you are likely to forget this information if you don't perform and repeat the actions as suggested above because when something new is learned, it must go straight into your memory bank or it's likely to be lost.

Obviously, if you're attending a class, it's unlikely that you will be able to repeat allowed what you want to commit to memory like you would in the introduction at a party example above, which is why taking quality and easy to follow notes emphasizing key words, thoughts, questions, and diagrams is so important. It's amazing how putting pen to paper really helps to lock new information into your memory.

Memory Techniques to Improve Recall, Learn Faster, and Build Long-Term Memory

It has always interested me, how some people seem to forget things all too easily, while others remain sharp as a tack. Genetics may play a part here, but I believe that it relates more to the choices we make. There are some simple things we can do that have been proven to sharpen and improve memory. As mentioned earlier, these include getting adequate sleep and giving the body regular physical exercise. Then there are the habits whose abstinence from can make a big difference as well. Smoking, drinking alcohol, eating processed foods, and reaching for the sugary snacks too often are all common examples of brain fogging habits that are best kept in check (or at least reduced). As well as being physically active, living a mentally active life is also pivotal. Mental exercises help keep the brain and memory toned and in tune.

There are different opinions when it comes to what sort of mental stimulation is best. The time-tested methods, like visualization and writing things down are still popular among many and for valid reasons. Then some modern techniques promise efficient results in building memory and improving cognitive functioning, facilitating us to learn things faster, stay focused, and mentally sound. As a rule of thumb, activities that push you to work beyond your comfort zone and require deep concentration are the ones to consider approaching. In the final section of this chapter, we look at both old and modern techniques and activities that serve as great exercises to improve memory and recall.

As you can appreciate, there are so many effective exercises and techniques in existence that, for the purpose of this book, I have selected and laid out a handful of my personal favorites for you to experiment with yourself. I have had the pleasure of teaching the following example exercises (ranging from the basic to difficult) and have seen some impressive improvements as a result.

Remember that to see substantial improvements in yourself, you will have to consistently practice the exercises over a period of several weeks. So, commit yourself and focus in, because results don't come from knowing how to exercise, they come from constant action taken over time.

Give them a try and see for yourself.

Visualization and Association Technique

Level: Easy

Some people seem to have photographic memories. If they set their eyes on something once, it gets stored in their memory forever. This is a unique ability to have and it's almost as if the people who have it were born with it. However, a similar skill can be honed, turning average memories into near-photographic memories. This is an age-old practice and yet, still one of the most popular one among memory performers. It is called the visualization and association technique (V&A). This technique helps with storing information as well as its retrieval and recall.

If you are one of those people who find it difficult to remembering specific details or find quick recall a real struggle, then I recommend practicing this technique daily as it can help you tremendously with both. You can use it to accurately recall almost anything, ranging from math formulas and lists to the dialogue from a script or speech.

The science behind this memorization technique establishes that the human mind usually takes in and hangs onto images and feelings (visual and kinesthetic) far better than verbal or written information. It's true. If I were to ask you to recall your childhood home's interior, a mental image will instantly form within your mind. You will tell me all about the visual aspects, the decor, your bedroom, or any other significant detail like all the fun you would have in your treehouse or pool in the backyard. However, if I asked you to recall the full home address of your childhood home you are likely to have a much tougher time. You will have to jolt your memory a little or might even have forgotten it altogether.

Images are concrete. Information is abstract. Creating visuals, especially of something that interests you, and then linking those visuals to information that you would like to lock into your memory is a great way to form a strong connection (a strong neural link). Using the visualization and association technique, you take in any abstract information and give it easy-to-remember mental images to go with. These images serve as mental story or hook and enable you to retrieve the information faster.

For example, if I asked you to memorize the following number sequence:

$$32 - 11 - 4 - 6 - 3$$

Then asked you to recall that sequence in order later today, it would be extremely tricky to say the least. Let's try to reframe the number sequence with a visual connection to something that you find interesting and ideally have an emotional tie to. Remember, as we discussed earlier in the goal setting chapter, emotion is stronger than logic.

Personally, I'm a big sports fan, so in this example I will try to link the numbers to a sport and build a simple, easy to visualize story to accompany it. Here goes!

There are 32 teams in the NFL and each team has 11 players on the field at a time. The game is made up of 4 quarters. Touchdowns are worth 6 points and field goals are worth 3.

It doesn't matter if you have an average or below-average memory, with this technique you can strengthen your neural connections, store information in your long-term memory easily, and recall almost anything accurately.

Write Things Down

Level: Easy

With the advent of computers and laptops and accompanying apps like planners, online calendars, notes, and snippets, we have put down our pens and stopped writing. Some studies suggest that writing things down using a pen/pencil is a faster way to encode the message and store it as a long-term memory. The physical act of writing stimulates the cells in your mind. This relates to one particular region in the brain called the reticular activating system. Every time the reticular activating system gets involved; the brain has to pay more attention to the action being performed. This was detailed in the book, *Write It Down Make It Happen: Knowing What You Want and Getting It* (Klauser, 2001, pp. 1–256) by Henriette Klauser.

Additionally, when you are writing by hand, your brain has to be more active in order to form each letter and word legibly. Some words require more hand movements than others and, therefore, the brain has to remain alert (Bounds, 2010). This isn't always the case when you type something on your laptop, as the only actions required type on a keyboard are the pressing of keys, rather than the almost artistic forming of word shapes when you write by hand.

Another study (Mueller & Oppenheimer, 2014) suggests that people who only take notes on a laptop end up just transcribing lectures verbatim. Conversely, when they write down notes by hand, they reframe ideas in their own words and thus, are more active learners.

In other words, by putting pen to paper and writing new information down in your own words, you'll have a far easier time of recalling that information when it is required.

Spaced Repetition

Level: Easy

According to one study conducted by researchers at the University of Texas, participants were asked to remember various magazine ads. The participants that were shown magazine ads more than once had better recall. This proved that repetition promotes the deep processing of information. The logic is simple. It is easier for you to recall something from yesterday as opposed to something from a week ago. Researchers refer to it as the forgetting curve (Challis et al., 1996). They believe that we forget newly acquired knowledge within a few hours or days. However, if we reinforce what we had learned at regular intervals, the brain is much more likely to retain that newly acquired knowledge for the long-term.

This technique strengthens your memory's ability to access information that you have encountered frequently, and it can happen either consciously (via memory training), or unconsciously (e.g. from ads on TV). Basically, this technique involves revisiting information that you wish to memorize, at regular intervals, in a variety of ways. Then by gradually increasing the time between revision intervals (you could start the intervals as hourly, then increase to daily, then weekly, and so on). When using this technique, I usually favor alternating between handwritten Cornell method notes and flash cards.

These notes and flash cards can be categorized by subject which makes this technique especially effective when preparing for something like an exam or job interview. Remember that like all training exercises, your best results will be produced by consistent repetition over time.

Chunking

Level: Medium

The act of chunking involves clubbing things together into groups. For example, if you are trying to learn the names of the greatest singers of all time, you can categorize them by genre, such as rock, rap, jazz, or pop culture. By placing the related information into groups, both learning and recalling the information is made far easier. Similarly, if you are preparing a grocery list, you can divide it into several smaller lists or groups like dinner items, clothing, breakfast things, or cleaning equipment. Thankfully, our brain is quick to recognize patterns and chunking items together helps it to store information more efficiently.

Music Mnemonics

Level: Medium

Music too can aid in revising and making things stick. It serves as a powerful mnemonic as it offers a pattern or sequence for information to be stored in the brain and encourages repetition. There is a reason why the brain can remember a catchy song from twenty years ago but has trouble recalling what you ate between lunch and dinner last Tuesday. Structuring information in a way that it can be remembered in the form of a song or jingle can is beneficial.

This method of memorizing is so effective at ingraining information into the mind quickly that even after years of constant use, it is still being utilized by marketers to plant desire for their products into your mind. If you take a moment to think about it, I'm sure that you can think of several product jingles that have locked themselves in your thoughts without you even realizing it.

Create a Memory Palace

Level: Difficult

This strategy is used by some of the top memory athletes. According to Roman legend, the memory palace technique was invented by Simonides of Ceos and favored by orators in ancient Greece as well as Rome. Also referred to as the method of Loci and the mind palace, the technique is both super effective and enjoyable. Interestingly, if you have had the chance to watch the modernized Sherlock Holmes series, you may have noticed that this is the technique that the character uses while recalling specific details and piecing together evidence when working on a case.

This method is not just reserved for consulting detectives, it can also be used to store and later recall the details of other things as well such as a speech you have to give or a list of names you have to remember. Nelson Dellis, four-time USA Memory Champion uses the memory palace technique. He claims to have had average memory to begin with but after training and developing this mnemonic technique, he has transformed himself into a memory recall and retrieval champion.

To begin using and developing this technique yourself, it's important to start out simple. At first, I recommend you use a location that you are familiar with. This place can be your apartment, a corner-side café you visit every day, your office, or even the route you take to go to work. Start out small and build your palace later. This method works by associating various points within the location you have chosen with the information that you would like to store and later recall. Imagine yourself visually pinning or placing representations of what you want to remember to positions within your chosen location.

To further elaborate. Let's assume that for now that your memory palace is your apartment.

Now, mentally walk through your apartment noticing any distinctive features you can use to encode what you want to remember. Every defined point that you stop on your imaginary walk through is a loci that you can pin or place the object or idea. For instance, start by walking through the front door to open your memory palace up in your mind. Then walk over to the couch, this can become your first loci. Then the TV console, which can be the second loci, the kitchen or the dining table can be the third loci, etc.

Now commit those features to your memory. When you think of the apartment, these objects and places will be imprinted in your mind.

Finally, associate what you need to remember or store, with the locus in your memory palace. For example, if you had a grocery list you wanted to memorize and the first item on the list was milk, you can associate it with the first loci by imaging milk flooding over the door like a waterfall. Similarly, if cereal was the second thing on your list, you can imagine your couch being replaced with uncountable cereal boxes neatly stacked over one another. Likewise, you can imagine your dining table has turned into a giant turkey with potatoes on each side of it.

When you try to remember things using this visualization technique, your memory improves. Every time you come across the door, you will be reminded of the milk. Every time you head towards the couch, the image of a cereal box will pop into your head. Every time you sit down to eat at the dining table, you will imagine the chairs as potatoes. It sounds almost like crazy talk, but it is a tried and tested way to supercharge memorization.

Each of these exercises comes backed by some scientific research. This is a clear indication that if we want to train the brain to become more open to new information as well as improve recall and learning speed, we can do so by implementing one or more of these into our daily regimes. Thankfully, they are simple and require no special instruments, to begin with. With some practice and some time, you will notice the improvement in your productivity, learning and memory retrieval abilities. You will find that more information sticks with greater ease, your focus becomes stronger, and your ability to retrieve valuable information becomes faster.

Summary

- They key to improving at anything is consistent practice combined with time.

- Put your thoughts and ideas into matching groups to help them stick.

- Use it or lose it. The quicker you use new information, the more likely you are to remember it. Think of the example given of how to remember a new acquaintance's name at a party.

- Your body and mind are part of the same powerful machine. To ensure optimum performance they must be taken care of. Remember that good nutrition, physical exercise, and the right amount of sleep will help you to level your up game.

- Visualization and association: Create a visual story in your mind and relate each step to something that interests you. Think back to the example of remembering a number sequence example by associating it with a sport.

- Go old school. Consider putting down the laptop and pick up a pen to paper. Writing well organized notes by hand and in your own words, helps you lock new ideas into your mind.

- When building a memory palace, start it off small and grow it over time.

- Train your mind a little each day and grow your memory like a muscle.

Chapter 3
Fall Down Seven Times
Get Up Eight

The title of the chapter is a famous Japanese proverb. It implies that one must get up when down and never give up, no matter how many times you fail. The number one reason we are afraid to try new things or tackle challenges is the fear of failure.

Fear, in itself, is a natural instinct. It is what allowed our ancestors to see and live another day. Had they not taken heed of their instincts and found cover when faced with a predator, they wouldn't have survived to tell the tale. Fear promotes survival. It is a gut feeling that prevents us from doing things that seem too dangerous or risky. You wouldn't want to dive into the waters from a cliff when you don't know what's at the bottom because you fear you might hit your head and drown. You don't go on a hike alone in the mountains because you know there's a possibility that a mountain lion might attack. You don't put your hand in a crocodile's cage at the zoo because you know it can bite your hand clean off. These examples are all self-preserving and rational. But more often than not, fear is totally irrational and stands in the way of achievement.

For example, fearing to share your ideas during a work meeting can hamper your chances of ever truly excelling. Fear of a breakup from your partner may keep you quite meaning you'll never address and resolve any conflicts. The fear of being bullied may be what prevents you standing up for what you believe is right at school or at work.

For centuries, the irrational fear of failure combined with negative self-dialogue has ruined lives. It has led people to believe that they will forever be average. Never rising because they are too afraid to take the necessary risks. It makes them play it too safe, suffocate their passions, give up on their dreams, and succumb to the harsh realities of life. I know that this may sound harsh, but the 'never try never fail' attitude is a genuine road to nowhere.

If the fear of failure (or fear of success which is equally destructive) prevents you from transforming your aspirations into reality, then this chapter is for you.

Let me be clear. Whether it is getting rejected by a romantic partner or flunking an exam, failure comes with no joy. For some, the fear is so real that they give up on their dreams altogether because they are not willing to (or don't know how to) put in the work that's required to bring their dreams to fruition. Have you ever sat down and thought about where these insecurities stem from? Is there a way you can leverage fear to your advantage?

People with a strong fear of failure, or atychiphobia, are practically paralyzing their chances of success. They believe that there is no point trying to achieve a goal unless there is an absolute guarantee of success. But this was never the intended purpose of fear. It was supposed to keep you alive, not make you surrender yourself and live an unhappy, unfulfilled, and unsatisfied life. Fear of failure can stem from traumatic experiences in the past. The trauma from those experiences or incidents can remain in the back of our minds continuing to affect us and every decision we make.

For example, you might have attempted to try something new and failed at it miserably, becoming the laughingstock of the family for the day. Even though your family probably didn't mean any harm, deep down that humiliation imprinted itself onto your mind, and from that day forward, every time you wanted to attempt something new or outside of your comfort zone, that little voice in your head reminded you of that moment of failure, along with all the feelings accompanying it, ultimately preventing you from taking action.

What's crazy about this is that when something like the example above affects you enough times, you can end up conditioning yourself to give up on what you want, before you even begin to try, and without even realizing why. If this remains unchecked, fear of failure or doubt in your own abilities can become something bigger than it should be and will hurt or even worse, kill your ambitions.

In Carol Dweck's book, *Mindset: The New Technology of Success,* she discusses failure and its impact. She talks about how some people never seem to learn from their mistakes because they have a fixed mindset. They believe that they don't have what it takes to be successful because they 'just weren't born with it'. Such people believe that things like intelligence, wisdom, and success are things some people are destined to have, and others aren't. They think that they can never succeed in their life goals, nor do they believe that they can develop and master the skills that they would need to achieve them. They are of the idea that they are already the finished product and there is no room for growth or improvement. This can make learning something new extremely difficult and step out of their comfort zone almost impossible because, in their head, there's no point.

On the other end of the spectrum are the people with a growth mindset or the winner's mentality. They believe that anything and everything is conquerable if they just believe in their own abilities and put their minds to it. They are willing to learn, progress, fail over and over, try again and again, and then eventually taste success. They are confident that if they put in the necessary work, they can achieve anything they set their eyes to. Their inner belief system is so strong, that when it comes to hitting a target or achieving a goal, they won't be denied.

That's the kind of mindset we need to develop, that winning attitude. That's what's going to help us overcome a fear of failure, regardless of whether it affects you a little or a lot. Let's reframe the way that we look at failing. Instead of thinking of it as absolute and throwing in the towel when it shows up, perhaps we can start to see it as a chance to test, learn and improve.

Read through the following list of questions and answer them honestly.

- Are you a frequent procrastinator?
- Do you suffer from low self-esteem and think that you are not good enough?
- Do you keep listening to, and believing every harsh judgement your inner critic makes, no matter how absurd?
- Do you have the habit of overthinking or exaggerating problems in your mind?

- Do you seek perfection in everything you do?
- Do you suffer from mental or physical performance anxiety?
- Do you play down compliments and constructive feedback because you think you don't deserve them?
- Do you talk yourself out of promising opportunities because you think you are unqualified?

If you answer yes to some of or all these questions, and can relate to these behaviors and traits, then it's a good indication that it's time to start making some changes. The first step to upgrading your mindset is to find out why you feel this why and determine what drives those behaviors in you.

Self-doubt is the killer of goals and dreams. There are many evidence-based studies showing that people often find it easier to give up on what they want to achieve, even when they're close, rather than compete or face a challenging situation. The fear of getting something wrong is a huge barrier to learning through action. It can be very demotivating and cause a lot of unnecessary stress, often because you don't want to look stupid to your peers who may later criticize.

There's a brilliant and quite apt piece of wisdom by the Chinese philosopher Lao Tzu which reads:

"Care about what other people think, and you will always be their prisoner."

- Lao Tzu -

The fear of what could happen ends up making nothing happen. In one report from the Global Entrepreneurship Monitor, 33% of would-be entrepreneurs never get their business off the ground because they are fearful, they might not live up to the mark. Many children don't take over their family's business when the time come, because they think that they are unqualified to do so and if they attempted to, they will never be able to fill the shoes of their forefathers. But how could they know that if they're not prepared to even try?

The impact of the fear of failure can't be underestimated. Not only can it stop us in our tracks, but it can also butcher self-esteem and motivation. With low self-esteem, it is impossible to step out of the comfort zone, because that negative inner voice keeps winning every argument you have with it. It says that you are incompetent, have zero chance of success and should therefore give up, which can make you lose all confidence in your abilities, skills, and knowledge.

It can be self-sabotaging and engage you in acts that undermine your chance of achieving success. It can cause shame and promote guilt. You don't want to feel ashamed or embarrassed and therefore, you question whether you should even try in the first place. This can further inflate a feeling of worthlessness.

Finally, it can snuff out your motivation all together. To achieve success at anything in life, you need the right driving force and the courage to commence. But if you never end up taking the first step because you don't have a compelling reason backing you or the right motivation fueling you, success becomes an impossibility.

How Our Internal and External Dialogue Shapes Our Mindset

The critical inner voice as briefly discussed is a well-integrated pattern of negative thoughts towards ourselves and others. They often come off as nagging voices or thoughts that create our internalized dialogue. The reason that learning to direct our internal dialogue is so important is that it shapes nearly all our behaviors, habits, and actions. If it is self-destructive, our actions will match.

In one study, researchers clocked the speed of inner dialogue and found that we have around 4,000+ words per minute spoken to us via our internal chatter (Korba, 1990). When compared with everyday speech, this is around ten times faster. The inner voice, often critical, is not an auditory hallucination. It often takes the shape of thoughts. Their stream forms an anti-self that is ready to put you down and discourage you from doing things that are in your best interest.

This negative self-dialogue often disguises itself as a concerned friend, but in reality, should be treated as an enemy. It has the power to overtake every aspect of our lives, including our decision-making and our ability to strive outside of the comfort zone to achieve our greatest goals. It toys with our confidence, our self-esteem, and seeks to destroy our personal and intimate relationships. These destructive thoughts can undermine our positive attitude and feelings about others and ourselves. They are famous for fostering inwardness, self-doubt, self-criticism, self-denial, distrust, and forces us to retreat from goal-directed activities.

Ever wondered where this inner voice comes from? How are these thoughts formed, and what experiences form them? Like fear of failure, these thoughts can stem from previous life experiences that have put us down in the past. Sometimes, these thoughts are external and come from our surroundings and the people in them, especially our parents, work colleagues or teachers. Sometimes, having unsupportive friends can also result in poor self-esteem and inwardness. These voices (especially when you're young) can come from interactions with influential adults or siblings who sense rivalry and therefore, it's easier for them to keep us down by putting us down, rather than putting in the work to lift themselves up.

Sometimes the negative inner voice designs a whole fictitious argument between you and another. In this scenario you can visualize the words, actions, and more importantly the feelings so clearly. You know that the words and actions from this hypothetical scene are made up and therefore fake, and after it has played out you move on. But it can be very difficult for your mind to filter out what you felt at that time, which can end up making those feelings stick around long after.

Before we move forwards, it's important to realize that everyone has experience of negative internal dialogue. It can be powerful and manipulative. Even though it plays with your emotions and is constantly trying to shape your actions, remember that you are more powerful. You're in control.

Taking control of your inner voice isn't a case of just trying to block out the negative. If you shut the doors on a voice that you no longer want to hear, it doesn't just go away. It will simply keep shouting obnoxiously louder until you can't ignore it anymore! A good way to start taking back control is to allow the thought to come into your mind, acknowledge it, calmly counter it with a positive truth and then let it pass. This way you can teach yourself to disregard any idea that belittles you or puts you down. It just takes a little practice, but trust me, once you have got the hand of it, it will become second nature and the confidence you have in yourself, and your abilities will grow.

There are a multitude of exercises that can help you to 'take control' and effectively shush the negative internal voice. But before we delve into those, let's look at the first step. I suggest that you start paying a little more attention to your positive internal dialogue (this may sound obvious, but it would amaze you how often this important step is overlooked). Even if it's sometimes difficult to hear, your positive inner voice is always there. We're all great at beating ourselves up if we make a mistake or miss the mark, but quite often we find it difficult to congratulate ourselves with a pat on the back after achieving a victory. Start by recognizing, rather than downplaying, your triumphs. Listen to what your internal dialogue sounds like now. This inner cheerleader or complementor is vitally important as it takes the reins and leads the counter arguments to all internalized negative talk.

Let's discuss three ideas that can help us improve our internal dialogue in a way that builds up self-esteem as well as the confidence to trust in our abilities. After we have looked at these, we can move on to some daily exercises that will help us overcome our irrational fears as well as take the power away from our inner critic.

Develop an Internal Complimentor

Our inner voice observes all our actions. It pays attention to our behaviors, goals, and ideas. For most people, this voice is like a punisher or whip that tells them that they aren't up to the mark. It keeps criticizing every effort, almost mocking them before they even begin.

If it feels like this is happening to you, pause and take note. What is it trying to tell you? If it is trying to put you down, it's time to activate the internal complimentor. Your internal complimentor has positive things to say about you, almost like a cheerleader but without the pompoms. This is not an exercise in lying to yourself, it's about remembering your goals, why you want to achieve them, how good you'll feel when you hit them, and the reasoning behind the actions you're taking to get you to where you want to be.

The internal complimentor supports your focus and helps you to keep your cool and continue moving forwards no matter what obstacles lay in your path. It reminds you of the times you've found strength, the greatness you're heading towards and how far you've come. And guess what, it even gives you a pat on the back just for acknowledging those truths.

Cultivate an Internal Motivator

A person's belief in themselves to tackle a situation or task is termed self-efficacy. It is closely linked to how persistent you are. You have to truly believe that you can handle a task or challenge because otherwise, you have already suffered defeat before you even begin which makes you either give minimum effort or worse still, not try at all!

Change the story in your mind from 'It's impossible for me' to 'of course I can do it'. This in turn changes the way that you approach any given situation. It helps to boost the confidence you have in your abilities by harnessing the internal dialogue that tells you that you can do anything you set your eyes on. Every time, you feel hopelessness creeping in, turn on your internal motivator, and get things moving.

A simple but surprisingly effective practice that helps harness and strengthen your internal motivator's dialogue is to repeatedly say to yourself 'I can do anything'. Try repeating this mantra to yourself 40 to 50 times each morning before starting your day. Sometimes say it aloud and sometimes in your head. In the mirror, look at yourself in the eyes while brushing your teeth and have your inner voice say it to you with conviction. Repeating a mantra to yourself is pretty old fashioned, but it really helps turn up the volume of your internal motivator.

Develop a Kind Tone with Yourself

As you get accustomed to the new way of talking and connecting with yourself, don't forget to be kind. Your internal dialogue should be humble. It shouldn't sound like a dictator forcefully barking orders at you. It should be patient, calm, and uplifting. Showing compassion towards yourself is extremely rewarding. Start to acknowledge all your accomplishments, whether they are big or small so that your inner critic can be silenced.

This is another example of using daily goals and daily scoring (as mentioned in an earlier chapter) as a motivator. Every time you hit a daily goal, take a second to acknowledge the achievement. Every day that you score a 9 or 10, congratulate yourself for your efforts. Remember that the seemingly small daily achievements compounded over time is what generates big, maintainable results. So, for every step forward you take, register it in a kind tone and a proud inner voice.

Changing the Way You Speak To Yourself

There is a profound Japanese proverb which reads:

"Don't speak bad of yourself. For the warrior within hears your words and is lessened by them"

- *Samurai* -

In other words, if you talk yourself down (even as a joke) these thoughts will eventually begin to take root in your mind, and you will start to believe them.

Right now, you must be wondering if it's even possible to change something that happens naturally without any conscious control or forethought. The good news is that science confirms that intentionally reshaping your thoughts can be done. It is possible with directed self-control. During one study, when participants were asked to inhibit negative thoughts, their brain activity showed a reduced movement in the amygdala. Amygdala is responsible for strong negative feelings. Moreover, increased activity was monitored in the prefrontal cortex which happens to be the center for emotional regulation (Cohen et al., 2016).

Try following these two simple exercises to give you a feel for how easily you can improve the way that your inner voice speaks to you. Just like with any exercise regime (both physical and mental) repetition and consistency of action is key.

The CBT Approach

Level: Easy

In this first exercise, you start with a pen and a sheet of paper. You can also use an Excel sheet or Google Spreadsheet for this. Whenever you feel down, demotivated, or have bitter feelings, use this approach to shift your focus from your inconsistencies and mishaps to something positive. This exercise is to help you come to terms with what's real and to disregard the exaggerated version presented to you by your inner voice's negative self-dialogue.

Name the first column as an automatic thought. This is where you will document all the negative thoughts that your inner critic presents to you or any fears that you have. You can choose to be detailed or keep it brief depending on what feels right at that moment. For example, your first automatic thought can be, 'My boss hates me' or 'I feel that I will be fired today.'

Once you have written it down, read it to yourself, and notice any reality distortions. Is it an exaggerated idea; is it the all or nothing mindset, mind-reading, overgeneralizing, catastrophizing, or something else? There can be more cognitive distortions at play than just one. In the statement above, we can count at least four of them at play such as mental filter, overgeneralization, jumping to conclusion, and all-or-nothing thinking. List this in the second column titled, cognitive distortions at play.

In the final column tilted, rational response, come up with a statement that is factual, and therefore logical. Once you have identified the cognitive distortions at play and understood that your fears are more than likely baseless, this should be easy. Using the above statement as an example, you could tell yourself that 'my boss doesn't hate me because if that were the case, he would have never asked me to lead the presentation', or 'I have had worse days than this and still wasn't fired. This is just a subpar day for me, and I will work harder tomorrow.'

You can do the same for every negative thought or fear you have inside you and conquer it with your rationale. Repeating this exercise will enable you to stop overthink and let things take their natural course before you go beating yourself up over thoughts that are usually not even based in reality.

The Positive Intelligence Exercise

Level: Easy

This comes recommended in Shirzad Chamine's book titled, *Positive Intelligence: Why Only 20% of Teams and Individuals Achieve Their True Potential and How You Can Achieve Yours*. Chamine has referred to the inner critic as the judge and talks about how easily we can discredit anything it has to say about us instantly. This is a great exercise for many reasons. First, it is simple and doesn't require any accompanying equipment. Second, it is ideal for all age groups and involves a few basic steps, and third, because you can perform it anytime, anywhere. He calls the inner critic's accomplice saboteurs. According to Chamine, the judge is extremely influential. It can propel us in judging ourselves and others. It also encourages comparisons with others, mostly with the ones that are more successful than us. It also doesn't stay behind in criticizing others or blaming circumstances.

Chamine believes that to take away the negative inner voice's power, we must first recognize the moments when we feel like criticizing or judging ourselves or others. As soon as we notice ourselves doing so, we must counter it with our inner voice by saying something like, 'there goes the inner critic again' or 'here we go, it's at it again'. Almost add a tone of voice to your counter where you can imagine yourself rolling your eyes as you say it. This discredits everything that it says afterward.

He also suggests that we must try to strengthen our 'sage brain' to consciously shift activity from our 'survivor's brain' to our empathy circuitry. This way, instead of comparing, blaming, or criticizing others, we can show empathy instead. This is possible to cultivate this with the help of some attention diverting exercises like deep breathing, tai chi, yoga, or anchoring in the present moment by focusing on our hands and feet.

Cultivating a Winner's Mindset

In 1910, on April 23rd, Theodore Roosevelt gave a speech that would become one of the greatest speeches of all time and go on to become one of the most quoted speeches of his career. It has come to be known as the "Citizenship in a Republic" or as some like to call it, "The Man in the Arena."

Touching on his own family, war, history, property rights, humans, and the responsibilities of citizenship, he railed against the pessimists that looked down upon men that were trying to make Earth a better place for all.

He started by talking about how the poorest way to face life was with a sneer on your face. He said that "A cynical habit of thought and speech, a readiness to criticize work which the critic himself never tries to perform, an intellectual aloofness which will not accept contact with life's realities—all these are marks, not ... of superiority but of weakness."

Next, he delivered words that were a wild success to the public. They became so popular that the bit ran in the *Journal des Debats*, was sent to teachers of France, printed by Librairie Hachette on Japanese vellum, and was turned into a pocketbook selling over five thousand copies in five days. It was also translated into different languages across Europe and shared with everyone that was a fan of the man.

It feels so inspirational that I didn't want to summarize or paraphrase it. Here's how it goes. You can read the complete transcript too:

"It is not the critic who counts; not the man who points out how the strong man stumbles, or where the doer of deeds could have done them better. The credit belongs to the man who is actually in the arena, whose face is marred by dust and sweat and blood; who strives valiantly; who errs, who comes short again and again because there is no effort without error and shortcoming; but who does actually strive to do the deeds; who knows great enthusiasms, the great devotions; who spends himself in a worthy cause; who at the best knows in the end the triumph of high achievement, and who at the worst, if he fails, at least fails while daring greatly, so that his place shall never be with those cold and timid souls who neither know victory nor defeat."

- Man in the arena speech - Theodore Roosevelt 1910, n.d. -

Such an awesomely motivating speech that is literally brimming with truths and wisdom. Perhaps read through it once more before continuing.

In short, it's ok to fail, as long as you are willing to get back up, dust yourself down, and go for it again. But having a winning mindset has much more to do with what's happening inside you. Remember, that the biggest obstacles aren't always external. They are created by the inner critic that wishes to see you stumble and give up, and then say, 'I told you so!'

You have to fight the negative version of yourself. That's the real challenge. You have to find ways to stem positivity within you and overshadow any doubting voices you may have lurking inside. If you have the right mindset, a challenge in the external world is nothing but a piece of cake. However, the goal here is to prevent your negative self from becoming someone that gets in the way of your champion self.

It all starts with what I like to call, auditing your thoughts. You can only build a winner's attitude if you know where you can and must improve. You also need to be clear on how you are going to improve. You see, it isn't just about knowing what you must do. You must know how you are going to do it. Perhaps, you need to check in with your accountability. Perhaps, you need to be careful of your inner dialogue and not pay attention to any negative things it says. Perhaps, you just need to work on following through on your word and promises. The real shift will happen when you intentionally choose activities and actions that test the very thing you want to work on and then overcome it.

A winning attitude isn't just a decision. It is a daily practice. The change won't happen overnight. It will take time and commitment. Your inner critic will challenge you at every step of the way, but you will have to fight it. If you want to truly know what cultivating a winner's mindset looks like, think of it as training for a boxing match. The more you practice, the stronger you will get at parrying and countering any harmful shots thrown your way. You will have to put in the time and effort and gradually grow. It's can feel like a slow grind at the time but it's worth the effort because with a little belief in yourself, you'll end up with a will of cast iron.

Winners know that achieving greatness has less to do with the destination and more with the journey. In fact, for them, the journey is usually more important. Even if you never arrive at your truly desired destination, the work that you put in along the way will shape you and your mindset into that of a winner. Keep in mind that no matter what your end goals are, success will never just magically appear. You will have to work like a warrior for it and that is only possible if you have a winner's mindset. Remember that winners aren't afraid to lose.

This was beautifully elaborated in Geoff Colvins' book titled, *Talent is Overrated: What Really Separates World-Class Performers From Everybody Else* (Colvin, 2019). He believes that the best performers set goals that are less about the outcome and more about the process of reaching the outcome.

Strongly believe that the next step, next opportunity, and the next commitment will work in your favor. You don't necessarily have to begin with high hopes. It starts with having faith in yourself. You must believe that you can do anything you set your heart and mind to. Only then, will you succeed.

Failure is our greatest teacher. Don't be afraid to try and fail because you can always go again. The truth is that the most successful people have failed the most times. What makes them achieve such amazing things is that they are always willing to get up one more time than they have failed.

Fall down seven times, get up eight.

Summary

- The fear of failure stands in the way of success.

- Self-doubt is a killer of achieving your goals.

- Internal and external dialogue shapes our mindset.

- Develop an internal complimentor and motivator.

- Change the way you speak to yourself. "Don't speak bad of yourself. For the warrior within hears your words and is lessoned by them".

- Failure is your biggest teacher.

- Winners aren't afraid to lose! The most successful people have failed the most times. Most of their success is a product of their unwavering perseverance. Never stop moving forwards no matter what obstacles lay in your path because a loss today can teach you what you need to succeed tomorrow.

- Cultivate a winner's mindset and become your own champion.

- Theodore Roosevelt's speech "The Man in the Arena" is excellent and motivating. It ties up this chapter nicely. Reread it from time to time to help realign your thoughts.

Chapter 4
Overcome the Beliefs That
Limit Your Progress

Our experiences shape most of our beliefs. We don't make conscious decisions about what feels right and what doesn't. Beliefs are based on generalizations of what we have been exposed to over a long period time. We are wired to hone in on what we have repeatedly seen, heard and experienced in the past and form either optimistic or pessimistic beliefs.

We have all had moments in life where we have blamed bad luck for something negative that has happened to us. We presume that we were destined to come across the mishap and there was nothing we could have done to prevent or avoid it. It is common to seek miracles to change conditions from 'bad' to 'good', without even considering the work that's clearly needed to get there.

Also, it's a fact that we give more attention to something bad that happens and seem to downplay or shrug off something good. If one thing goes wrong, we keep dwelling on it the whole day. We come up with further past experiences to back up our stories of why we can't get out of something, solely because we have believed in it for too long.

This personal narrative can prevent us from doing things we should be doing to move forward. It prevents us from achieving our goals and true potential. Even though we know that we can improve the quality of our lives by learning and mastering something new, our limiting beliefs and self-doubt, if fueled, either stand in the way obscuring our path ahead or end up stopping us in our tracks entirely. The reason this happens is that limiting beliefs determine the actions we take, and the actions we take affect the results we achieve and the speed in which we attain them. If we start a journey with a pessimistic attitude, don't put in the work, and then finally don't achieve the desired results, it reinforces a belief that it just can't be done. Simply put, we can be our own worst enemy.

Tony Robbins once said, "The only thing that's keeping you from getting what you want is the story you keep telling yourself."

If you keep telling yourself that you don't have it in you to achieve your biggest goals, you will begin to believe it, I've always thought that this Henry Ford quote sums it up nicely "Whether you think you can or you think you can't, you're right".

Psychologist Robert M. Williams in his research paper describes limiting beliefs as the filters of a camera (Fannin & Williams, 2012). We see what the camera shows us with the filter on. In other words, how we see things is a function of our beliefs. It shapes our personality. We feel worthless, powerless, incompetent, an outcast, or undeserving of any success in all walks of life.

Limiting beliefs stop movement and progress. They make us question things with a negative attitude. Such beliefs are usually triggered because of specific episodes in the past where we were told that we weren't deserving or competent enough to do something. In his book, Dr. Bruce Lipton states that most of the beliefs are formed by the time we turn seven. During the first few years of our lives, we are like sponges, taking in everything–the good and the bad (Lipton, 2016). "How will you join the basketball team if you can't even catch a ball properly?"

Such statements can find a home in the brain and stay with us forever. Every time we want to give something new a try, our brain replays the memory in our subconscious mind and deters our actions. It also breeds procrastination, anxiety, conformism, overthinking, and imposter syndrome.

You can develop limiting beliefs about yourself, others, and the world. You believe that something is inherently wrong with you, you feel that others are out to get you, or you think that the universe is playing against you.

Some common examples of limiting beliefs include:

- I'm not good enough.
- Nobody likes me.
- I'm a failure, so why even try.
- Why am I so awkward?
- I have no control over the situation.
- If I go for my goal, I might end up alone.

The first step to overcoming a limiting belief is to identify which one is dominant in your life. This calls for a blame-free analysis where you identify the instances, triggers, and patterns of limiting beliefs and resonate with them.

Blame-Free Analysis

We have all set New Year resolutions only to give up on them a couple of weeks later and blame our lack of willpower. The cycle begins again the next month or the next year, and the story repeats itself. If you can connect with that, know that there is a self-limiting belief in action that is holding you back. A blame-free analysis allows us to lay the blame aside and analyze what went wrong and how to overcome the hurdle next time.

Here are some questions to ask yourself:

- Were the goals realistic to begin with?
- If they were, what stopped you from achieving them? Was it external pressure, your lack of willpower, both or something else?
- Is there something you could have done differently?
- If yes, why didn't you do it the first time? Were you unsure of the outcome it might yield and are you willing to try again?
- Are there any obvious behavior patterns you can observe? Which of these do you think prevent you from taking action?
- Do you tell yourself a back story to feel better about situations?

Continue to probe questions without any judgments or blame. This is an important step as it helps you identify the reasons why something didn't go as planned. Take notes and analyze what should be done next. Ask yourself that if you were given another chance how would you turn the situation in your favor?

Once you identify the limiting beliefs that are obstructing you, the next step is to learn some ways to overcome them.

Understand what purpose it serves

Each limiting belief serves a purpose. The reason you might fail at something repeatedly or give up could be because you're seeking perfectionism. You want things to be done at the perfect time, in ideal conditions and in an error-free way first time. So, when the timing isn't perfect and conditions aren't favorable, you opt to call it quits because you don't want to be average or lower.

However, if you think about it, there is rarely a perfect time or ideal conditions to do something, and if you're trying something new, then of course you're going to make some errors to begin with. Remember that mistakes (or failures) are one of our greatest teachers, as long as you're willing to learn from them. Realize this and you will be able to progress towards your goals quickly.

The limiting belief of perfectionism is the example of purpose here. Find yours.

Question your Beliefs and Visualize Success

As soon as you have identified the purpose of the limiting belief; question whether it is a valid belief or not. Visualize what you want and how it feels once you achieve it, whether you're learning a language, a musical instrument, or your timetables, it doesn't matter what you're working towards. Tell yourself that you can achieve anything that you plan for and work towards. Believe inside your heart that you won't be denied your goal and your path ahead will become clear.

Face Your Fear of Failure

As discussed earlier, the fear of failure is yet another common limiting belief. It is natural to feel unsure and suffer from anxiety, but if this keeps encouraging you to give up before you even begin, or if it becomes your consistent state, this needs to change. Fight the negative emotions hinder your actions or hamper your behavior. Take back control of your self-belief and what you want to achieve by engaging in daily exercises that were mentioned in the previous chapter to get started.

Retrain Your Brain

The brain can be retrained, thanks to neuroplasticity. Beliefs are nothing but patterns that the brain has already identified. This can be rewired by introducing a new pattern in its place and by repeating the new action until it becomes a habit. You can do so in many ways like repeating positive affirmations to yourself or carrying something in your pocket that reminds you of your new intentions. You can develop good habits that will eventually, make room for and promote new beliefs to form.

Develop a Growth Mindset

As discussed earlier, a growth mindset propels you to expand on your existing skills, become proficient in your abilities, and encode new knowledge. If you have trouble with a limiting belief, you can try to focus more on the possible solutions and learn to improve instead of just giving up and blaming your luck. Having a fixed and unchangeable mindset, will always make this difficult. Those who believe that they can learn from their mistakes to improve their future performance, believe in themselves, their abilities and always find a way to become successful in what they do.

Don't Forget to Celebrate Small Wins

Every once in a while, look back at your journey and give yourself some appreciation for how far you have made it so far.

Learn to pat yourself on the back for a job well done. So many people only see the mistakes they have made and don't spend time celebrating the successes that they have achieved. Remember we talked about how just one bad thing can ruin an otherwise brilliant day? Celebrating every small win and success can prevent that kind of negativity finding its way in and clouding your mind.

We all have internal arguments going on all the time; just make sure that the self-doubting inner voice is always countered with the internal voice of reason that wants you to attain success in everything you do. You can do so by setting small goals that can be fulfilled throughout the day, this will help you to change your perspective. Find reasons why you want to challenge a certain belief by breaking down where it stems from as well as how and why it affects you. Then, step by step, take action by setting short-term goals to stay focused and motivated.

Summary

- Destiny is not set, you create it yourself.

- "Whether you think you can or you think you can't, you're right" (Henry Ford) | The lesson here is always think you can, even if you have to learn a new way.

- Practice blame-free analysis to help identify and plan to overcome limiting beliefs.

- If you're willing to learn from them, your failures can become one of your most valuable teachers.

- Dig into and identify what you believe the purpose of your limiting belief serves. This will give you the insight to either tackle or dismiss it.

- Face the fear of failure. Develop a growth mindset and visualize success.

- Remember to acknowledge and celebrate all your wins. Even the small ones!

Download your goal setting and reference notes from:
bit.ly/howtolearnfasterbook

Chapter 5
7 Steps to Faster Learning

We all learn in different ways and at a different pace. You can't compare how one's mind comprehends new information, how much time it takes to encode it, how it is stored in the brain, and later retrieved. In truth, retrieval defines how the information comes into use later. Even if some of us have encoded the message successfully, it isn't guaranteed that the message finds its way home in our long-term memory. Science tells us that the relationship between a student's learning and the hours invested is more intricate than we think.

Research doesn't fully support the idea that if we spend more hours studying, we will automatically learn and retain more. This means that you may fritter away a 20+ hour block of studying and end up pulling an all-nighter, without even necessarily grasping the basic concepts of the material. In contrast, a friend of yours who studied for 5 hours or less, seems to be more equipped with the knowledge. You may feel that you don't have enough to show for the volume of time you spent revising. Why does this happen? It is a possibility that when you go to a lecture, lesson or seminar and come out with nothing significant to discuss or revise from. It's also possible that the time you spend revising is more comparable to that of a scatter gun rather than a well thought out plan.

How someone learns and at what pace involves several important factors. Think of it as a blend of the right learning resources available, previous knowledge of the subject, learning abilities, motivation levels, learning opportunities, peer pressures, and so on. In the not too distant past, teachers and educators weren't able to tailor the learning material provided or adapt their approach towards each student. Thankfully, today, teachers are more involved in helping students cope with their different learning levels and fill in any gaps with their commissioned teaching approaches.

Speaking of learning at a different speed, you don't need to look further beyond your friends, class mates or work circle to spot the differences in how each of you assimilates new information. Some of you might find it easy to read and absorb long pages of information, whereas others find them indigestible. They are more visual or auditory learners. Then some have poor attention spans and are easily distracted when it comes to study, whereas some become so engrossed in the lectures that they fail to take note of all that is going on around them. They wouldn't know what time of the day it is, and whether they had eaten or not. Some have to find a quiet spot to concentrate, while others enjoy being taught with a little background noise going on.

Whichever learning style you feel most comfortable with, you can always improve the way you take in and remember information using the 7 simple steps discussed in this chapter. Even if you are the most advanced learner, or if you find study a struggle, following these steps to the dot can help you to substantially up your game. They will assist in encoding information faster, making and sticking to a schedule, and will help you to track your progress in real-time.

Even though some of these steps may seem like common sense, you should be honest with yourself about whether or not you actually go through them when you study. In my experience I have found that just because something may seem to be obvious, it doesn't necessarily mean that it's being done.

Step 1: Empty Your Cup

The first and possibly the most important step is to 'empty your cup'. Mentioned below is one of the most self-taught stories of all times and is relatable to so many fields of life. It is derived from an old Chinese Zen proverb, "empty your cup". There are many different versions of this tale, but let's stick with a basic one that highlights the relevant core message.

The story begins with a master trying to teach his student *(the scholar Tokusan)* about the fundamentals of Zen. The student, however, wasn't a beginner. He already had some experience regarding the subject. Therefore, each time the master tried to teach the student something new, the student would compare the master's teachings with his own preconceived notions and beliefs, and as a result, was unable to truly understand the lessons that the master was trying to teach him.

Finally, the master stopped and poured himself a serving of tea, followed by a second full serving of tea for his student. The master then said that he would like to share some of the tea from his own cup with the student and started to pour. But the student's cup was already full, and all the tea that the master poured into the student's cup spilled out onto the surface below.

The student said "Stop master, my cup is already full. Every drop that you try to pour in is being wasted". To this, the master replied, "You're exactly right. Your cup is so full that nothing more can fit". The master smiled and then continued "You are like your cup. So full of ideas that there is no room for anything new". After a moment's thought, the student realized that he had so many preconceived beliefs about Zen teeming in his mind, that there was no room for him to truly understand the master's lesson. The master paused, and then in a calm tone explained that if he wanted to seek new knowledge, he must first learn to empty his cup.

A look of enlightenment dawned on the student, followed by a smile. He seemed more receptive this time. Looking at his expression and his willingness to learn, the master began his lesson again.

I love how this story shows with such simplicity that if you are aiming to take in and retain information about a new subject at speed, you must first fully open your memory banks by removing information obstructions, such as any pre-conceived or half-baked ideas you may have, before you begin.

Step 2: Take Action

Taking action is an important part of retaining what you have learned. You must put the newly received knowledge to use as soon as possible or else bits of it will begin to disappear from your memory. This takes us back to when we talked about building your memory like it is a muscle. The more you practice, the more efficient you become. Similarly, the sooner you use your newly acquired knowledge, the quicker you can commit it to your long-term memory. Quality repetition is everything here.

But how can you take some big action right away when you are still in class, or when you have to spend hours at a seminar before going home? The simple answer here is to take high quality notes. Taking detailed notes will help reduce the time you need to spend on revisions and editing. Rather than just writing down word for word what was being said at the time without really absorbing the new information, notes should be taken in a way where key points trigger what you have already stored in your memory. This makes understanding the information during the lesson easier to follow and the revision of the information at another time faster. There's a reason that ultra-successful people, such as Sir Richard Branson, keep a written journal. Putting things down on paper, whether in the traditional or contemporary method, locks new information into the mind.

You might think that taking your notes on a laptop is more efficient and easier to study from. I suggest you think again. In my opinion, pen and paper will forever be the most powerful note-taking method. Research has proven it to be the quickest and easiest way to learn, comprehend and retain new information. In one study at Princeton University, researchers found that students that took notes by hand were more actively engaged in the lecture. They found it easier to recall what they had been taught later on and also had their concepts clear. On the other hand, the students that took their notes by typing on a laptop had multiple errors in the transcription and seemed more distracted. They also had a difficult time recalling what they had been taught in class.

To be sure, three different studies were conducted during the experiment with different sets of students and each study proved that students that took notes on their laptops performed poorly on conceptual questions compared to those that had taken notes by hand. They proposed that although taking notes via laptop seemed easier, processing of information slowed down. Students also had trouble reframing concepts into their own words which is a crucial part of the learning process. Handwritten notes improve comprehension and retention of new information, because the brain has to be more attentive while taking them.

If you would like to push your note-taking skills to the next level, the following chapter is going to be of great interest to you as it discusses several highly effective techniques.

Step 3: Optimize Your Learning State

The next thing to focus on is how your posture influences your state of mind. A lot of people underestimate the importance of an appropriate posture when they learn, but it is believed that it plays a crucial role in the way the mind absorbs information. For example, if you are slouched in your chair with your head leaning on your hand, it signals the mind that you are either bored or that the information being presented to you is unimportant. If this is the case, you will have a hard time focusing and assimilating the new information effectively. Conversely, if you sit upright, poised, and ready to listen, your mind will follow suit and remain alert and in the state of attention. You will find it far easier to focus as your posture will keep you engaged and wanting to take in more.

Your body's nervous system acts as a secondary brain. What you do at any given time with your body's position and posture has a direct impact on your state of mind. Let's use a fun example of how you prepare yourself for sleep. If you want to go to sleep, you lay down and close your eyes. This makes falling to sleep natural and inevitable. What if you changed your position by sitting up and then only closed one eye? Now falling asleep is still possible but unlikely. Finally, what if you change your body position further, stood up and opened both your eyes? Now, unless there's an underlying medical condition, falling asleep is impossible! I realize that this example seems ridiculous, but I think that it is a fun and easy way to understand how what you do with your body position, directly affects what you do with your mind.

An alert body makes for an alert brain. Some studies link physical exercise with your ability to absorb new information. In the book, *Spark: The Revolutionary New Science of Exercise and the Brain*, Dr. John J. Ratey, an associate clinical professor at Harvard Medical School, writes that exercise remodels the brain to work at its optimal on all fronts. He proposes that exercise improves the process of learning on three levels.

1. It augments your mindset by improving alertness, motivation, and attention.
2. It promotes the binding of nerve cells with one another, which is essential when you are trying to log in new information.

3. It encourages the development of new nerve cells from stem cells, produced in the hippocampus.

This means that not only does physical exercise promote learning, it also encourages retention. In another study, researchers at a suburban school district in Illinois introduced an early morning exercise regime for students called the Zero Hour. They wanted to learn whether students would perform better after working out before starting school. The findings revealed that nearly all the students showed a boost in their reading ability and in all subjects. Ever since the program was introduced, teachers and educators report a remarkable improvement in the academic performance as well as wellness of all students (Barile, 2017).

Try not to get yourself worked up about working out. Exercise doesn't always have to mean hitting the gym hard. It can be as simple as taking a brisk 15 minute walk before you begin your study or during a break.

Step 4: Create A Learning Schedule and Stick with It

It's important to spend some time planning out a study schedule in advance rather than just going at it ad hoc. Getting this simple but essential learning schedule right has been proven to greatly increase study speed which in turn increases productivity. The best way is to start with a set schedule that lists all the activities, tasks, and chores that you are expected to finish. Take each of these tasks, activities and pieces of learning material and put them into an order of urgency and importance. Then arrange it so that the first task that you tackle each day, is the most challenging.

Working on the 'worst tasks first' while your mind is fresh has a big positive psychological effect. You feel a big sense of accomplishment early on in your study session and the thought of the rest of the planned agenda getting easier after completing the first task is quite motivating.

Although you might be tempted to schedule an entire month in advance, let's focus on one week of learning at a time. This prevents the structure being rigid and allows you to adapt it by adding extra tasks or changing the order of importance as the weeks progress. If you find the routine workable, you can repeat it the following week and so on.

Having a well-structured learning schedule helps to keep you on target, keeps your concentration aligned with your goals and prevents procrastination. It promotes faster and more focused learning because rather than thinking "what should I work on next" or just working vaguely on a particular broad subject, you follow an order and set aside time solely for a particular part of a subject which then leads into another. This (similarly to the daily goals) gives you a check list that you can very satisfyingly check off as you go, which in turn fuels your motivation. Following an organized agenda, helps cultivates the habits you need in order to keep moving forward.

Keep in mind that this isn't about dragging yourself through endless hours of continuous studying every single day. You just have to commit yourself to following your agenda to the letter by working on the preplanned tasks, at their allotted time slot, for the predetermined amount of time. When you begin your study slot, ensure that you put your smartphone facedown and on silent mode so that you aren't tempted to check your emails or fall into the time wormhole of social media. Furthermore, find yourself a comfortable and distraction-free spot where the TV won't entice you to watch.

Humans have a limited attention span. Depending on the individual, the brain can only concentrate between approximately 45 and 90 minutes at a time before focus wanes. I believe that study slots should be kept to around the 50 minute mark to keep the brain working at its optimum rate. Take a 5 to 10 minute study break between scheduled slots to allow your mind to rest and recover before you get back to it. Go for a short walk, stand in the garden, or even complete a short household chore in this time will further help to relax your mind. Ideally refrain from any information onslaught such as scrolling through the endless feeds of social media during this time as it doesn't give your mind the opportunity to rest and can end up leading to procrastination when you get back to work.

Let's start out easy. Dedicate 2 x 50 minute unmovable study blocks per day to your calendar for the next seven days. To build a strong and positive habit, you have to stay consistent so that the brain has the chance to become accustomed which will make it feel natural. Mark the time on your calendar and set a reminder for it.

I believe in keeping a written journal containing my daily and weekly agenda whenever I am learning a new subject or training to master a new skill. I find that striking off each accomplished action as soon as they are complete really helps keep my eyes on the prize and my motivation fired up. The idea here is to make the study agenda realistic, but not easy. If you make it way too easy, you probably will not take your sessions seriously which can lead to you forgetting about your goals and stopping. If you're repeatedly over ambitious with what you set yourself to complete in your agenda, you may well become demotivated and give up. Play around with it to begin with until you can get it just right.

Use the first few weeks of trialing this method as a practice phase where you can experiment and find out what study time slots and work volumes etc. work best for you. And what tracking method (such as journaling) helps you work at your most motivated.

Step 5: Talk the Talk

Discussing newly learned information with fellow students and colleagues is a great way to reinforces your own understanding of it. Talking through concepts with others and explaining to them in your own words has been shown to help further your comprehension of these new ideas, as well as strengthen your ability to memorize them. This is one reason why group studies are common among young adults and college students. Everyone bringing their perception to the table can create room for better understanding as well as improve recall.

This was further explored by researchers in a study whose basic premise was to establish a connection between improved memory recall and teaching (Nestojko et al., 2014). It reveals that when we teach others what we know, it encourages us to come up with better and more creative approaches. You can explain things using various examples that aid locking the information in your brain. In other words, the act of teaching others, builds your own memory.

Teaching others or merely speaking to them about the things you know also greatly improves your confidence level with regard to the subject. This is called the protégé effect. It is a psychological phenomenon that states that teaching others or even pretending to teach others (e.g. practicing in an empty room or in front of the mirror) helps with the absorption of information. Any student studying for an exam, interview, or thesis can use the protégé effect to quickly improve their understanding. Several benefits to it come backed by science.

For example, teaching or practicing to teach, leads to improved metacognitive processing (Muis et al., 2016). This results in active awareness of the learning process, resulting in increased concentration and focus. Then, teaching others or talking to them leads to increased use of learning strategies. You will also feel more motivated to learn because you are expected to teach others (Chase et al., 2009). Teaching others or 'pretending' to teach others facilitates your ability to learn the material well. Students and employees that spend more time trying to perfect their concepts through talking to others about them perform better when tested on the material.

Additionally, let's not forget that the benefits aren't just limited to an academic setting. We can all improve learning and boost memory by teaching others in practically any field.

Step 6: Create Mental Pictures

Creating vivid mental images or models, much like we discussed earlier with the memory palace example, is a great asset when committing information to the long-term memory. It doesn't always have to be quite as extravagant as the memory palace technique, it can be simplified down to picturing a photo or diagram in order to lead you into remembering the specific details or information that you link to it. Visual learning has always been a brilliant medium for teaching children. It is equally as effective to aid adults with their retention of knowledge and speed of recall.

Mental imagery or visualizing pictures in your mind triggers linked memories in a similar way that it would if you were looking at something that is right in front of you. How often have you flicked through a photo album, either on your phone or in a book, and seen a picture of a place that you had visited on holiday years ago that you had practically forgotten about and as soon as you see a single picture, all of the memories surrounding and relating to the holiday seem to come flooding back into your mind? Details that you would have not been able to recall without the visual aid. Where you ate your lunch, who said what and that funny thing that happened. You get the point.

Using visuals to memorize information helps to improve your planning and anticipation. Think back to when we discussed setting goals. Visualizing what you wanted to achieve and why made it far easier to plan how to get there. Even when we are in the middle of another task, visualizing an image allows us to recall the associated information with greater ease. Mental visualization plays specific roles in the thought processes, such as problem-solving, direct memory, decision-making, and motor control tasks.

Step 7: The Importance of Sleep

It might seem unrelated to learning or improving memory, but there is a strong correlation between your mind and your sleep. In simple terms, having the 'proper' amount of sleep allows the brain some time to process all your memories from the day. In this downtime, your mind is still working to file everything away so that the information can be retrieved later.

Unsurprisingly, studies have revealed that sleep affects your academic performance (Okano et al., 2019). As mentioned, sleep is the time when most of the consolidation of memory takes place. This is one reason why several studies promote the idea of taking a short siesta during the daytime (especially if you find it difficult to take your full block of sleep in one go) to help you recharge and be more productive. During one study (Read, n.d.), participants were asked to test their memory strength by memorizing illustrated cards. After the illustration of cards, both groups were told to report back after a 40-minute break. The first group was told to take a nap, while the other group was told to stay awake. After the 40-minute break, they were tested again on the memory of their memory. As it turned out, the group that took a nap performed better at recall. Factually, they were able to retain an average of 85% of the patterns on the set of cards compared to the second group that only retained 60% of the information.

Another study looked at the connection between sleep deprivation and our ability to commit new information into memory. The findings reveal that those who suffer from poor sleeping habits have a hard time pushing information into long-term memory (Yoo et al., 2007). At this point it's also worth mentioning that a good amount of sleep, as well as sleep deprivation for that matter, compounds. What I mean by this is that if you are an hour behind on your sleep each night for five nights in a row, and then you have an extra two hours sleep on the sixth night, you still owe yourself three hours sleep for your brain (and your body) to run at it's optimum. By the way, the 'proper' amount of sleep per night slightly varies from person to person. The National Sleep Foundation guidelines advise that a healthy adult should have between seven and nine hours of sleep per night, children require more as they're bodies as well as their minds are growing.

All these studies prove the importance of sleep as well as a consistent sleep schedule. As students or employees, schedule sleep times and stick to a sleep routine. This will help your brain and your body's circadian clock to sync. On top of this, there are so many other obvious and hidden benefits to getting a good night's sleep ranging from, the positive impact in your mood and temperament, to an improvement of your concentration levels. All of the benefits combined will ultimately help you to learn things much faster.

Even looking at sleep on a physical level. If you have exercised your body in the day, your muscles will be given more of a chance to develop quicker, if you're giving them enough sleep to recover properly. So, trust me when I say, there is nothing on late night TV or Netflix that will upgrade your brain and improve your life as much as the sleep that you're missing out on if you watch.

Since I am a big fan of Jim Kwik, I think his FAST technique will make for the perfect end to this chapter. Kwik has over 25 years of professional experience and has worked closely with some of the world's greatest minds, CEOs, executives, athletes, students, celebrities, and super achievers to help them train their brains to fitness. He is a well-celebrated brain coach who has developed world-class accelerated learning programs to enhance brain performance.

Here's a short summary of what Jim's *FAST* technique stands for.

The F stands for forgetting. Kwik suggests that if we want to speed up the process of learning, we must forget three things. First, we must forget our preconceived ideas about something. If we already have a basic knowledge of the subject, we must clear it from our mind and start from the beginning. He calls the mind a parachute that only works when it's open. He believes that one of the most common barriers to learning is people thinking they already know a lot about the subject. Think back to the Zen master's wisdom discussed earlier and 'empty your cup'.

The second thing he wants us to forget is trying to multitask. He stresses that we forget about all those things that are neither urgent nor important. He states that one can't expect the brain to fully engage in active learning if it is at four different places at once.

The third thing he asked that we forget about is our limitations. Believing that you have 'always been a slow learner', or 'lack the right tools to educate yourself' and you will continue to hamper your process of taking in new information. You need to fight these limitations and enable yourself to develop a growth mindset.

The A stands for Active. Kwik believes that we can't process information effectively if we are lectured to but are not engaging. We process information when we are an active part of the process. He stresses taking your sweet time to consume new information because the process of learning and memorizing is not a spectator sport. You must ask more questions, take better notes, and become fully engaged in the process of learning.

The S stands for the state. The mental and physical state that you are in when taking in the new information matters a lot. Our state of mind is a snapshot of our body and mood. If we feel emotionally unavailable at any given moment, it becomes hard to fully grasp something. For example, if you are in some form of pain or discomfort, you will be distracted due to it. Once you feel physically and emotionally well, you can commit new information to long-term memory. Kwik believes that one of the many reasons that some of us found it difficult to effectively learn at school, was because the umbrella emotion felt was boredom. We felt bored because we were verbally lectured at all day by different teachers. There were fewer audiovisual aids to make subjects and learning material more interesting.

However, Kwik reminds his followers that the state of your mind is in your control. You can choose to improve this state whenever you want to by taking a few deep breaths, changing your posture, and remind yourself of why you're there and the benefits of the information you are receiving. If you enter a classroom or seminar with a joyous, curious, and fascinated mind, learning will come easily.

Finally, the T stands for teach.

Kwik suggests that if you wish to cut your learning curve in half, you must learn it to teach it to someone else. If you were to give a presentation about what you learned today in class, you would learn differently. You would be more attentive. You will take better notes. You will remain alert and active throughout the lecture. You would ask better questions too. When you change the intention of why you are learning, you change the way the information gets absorbed in the mind. The reason he stresses that we share and talk about what we learned with others is that it allows us the opportunity to learn twice.

Summary

- 'Empty your cup' – forget what you think you know about a subject before you begin.

- Take action – Use what you have learned to lock it in.

- Optimize your learning state – If your posture looks like your interested in something, your mind will follow suit.

- Create a learning schedule and stick with it – Pre book your study blocks and be accountable.

- Talk the talk – Discuss or even better teach newly learned information to improve your own understanding.

- Create mental pictures – Clear visualization massively improves the ability to store and recall detailed information.

- The importance of sleep – Try to get your 7 to 9 hours per night to improve both your body and mind. It's understandable that this is not always possible (especially as a parent). If this is the case, try starting out small, and aim to get to bed 20-30 minutes earlier than usual. This extra little bit of rest time compounds into an additional 2 to 3 ½ hours per week!

Download your quick reference chapter notes from:
bit.ly/howtolearnfasterbook

Chapter 6

Next Level Note Taking

As I'm sure you already realize, note-taking is an essential study tool, and when utilized correctly greatly improves memory recall and how you push things into your long-term memory. We all usually start taking notes in high school and might think that it's as simple as writing down as much as possible. This way of thinking may not necessarily be wrong, but to get the most out of the active learning experience of a live lecture and still end up with a set of awesome notes to study from is somewhat of an art form. This becomes even more prevalent when you start college and are introduced to back-to-back scheduled lectures where there are hundreds of students like you. The teachers, although helpful and welcoming, expect you to note down lectures so that you can prepare for your final exams. The way knowledge is dispersed changes. There are fewer textbooks involved from where you can cram texts and write them down in the exams. The emphasis lays on your shoulders. The exams are less likely to ask for a definition straight out of a book. The questions demand in-depth analyses and conceptual answers based on your own understanding.

Hopefully this helps you to see what I mean, because learning an effective note-taking method should be seen as both a necessity and an art. If you would like to improve your note-taking ability, then you're in the right place. In fact, even if you are a super proficient note taker, it is still worth seeing if you can push your skill level up a notch. I would like to clarify one thing here before we begin. Note-taking, in any way, isn't about just putting your head down and simply filling up page after page, word for word. It shouldn't take away the focus from the actual learning. The purpose of a set of awesome notes is to take you back to what you have already actively learned. Without the connection between your stored memory of what you have actively learned and your notes, you will miss out on the context of what you have written and will more than likely end up with a bunch of pages that mean very little. Effective note-taking is about taking down key elements that spark the memory of the live lesson, the live seminar, the book, the YouTube video, or whatever.

Although there are countless excellent note-taking techniques in existence, I would like to talk about the four, which I not only use myself, but that I believe are some of the easiest to grasp and use straight away. Of course, like all things, the following methods require a little effort and focus to begin with, but when you have them down to a T, they will become second nature to you. If you can adopt some of, or all of these strategies, they will greatly assist you on your learning journey.

Let us begin.

The Outline Method

The first note-taking style that I would like to discuss with you is called the outline method. I find this one to the easiest to grasp and is also one of the most common note-taking method used which makes it a good place to start. You might be adhering to some of this method's rules without even realizing it. This method allows for a structured organization of your thoughts and ideas which helps with reducing the time needed for reviewing and editing later on.

To utilize the outline method, use bullet points to note down important ideas and thoughts during a lecture or webinar. Each bullet point introduces a new thought. Every important topic that is being introduced is placed farthest to the left of the page. Under each heading, subtopics will be added, indented a little to the right to denote that they are an expansion of the same idea. Try to use key phrases and words rather than writing down reams and reams of text.

If there are more supporting subtopics, they are added below, indented further towards the right side of the page. This forms a simple to follow and organized structure which really helps when you review and revise from your notes in the future.

Being the simplest note-taking method featured in this book, this is exceptionally efficient and reduces the amount of time you spend writing when you should be watching and listening to what's being taught. This means that you will have more time to grasp the topics discussed at the time that they are being learned, which will help you, with the aid of your notes, to mentally recall the rest if the related information later.

You can improve on your original design and add more arrows and lines to form strong links between concepts and ideas as well as differentiate between multiple topics. You can also add colored sticky notes as topic dividers to keep sections quick to locate. Also try adding any important, memory sparking key words or comments in the page's margin as this will help you with visualizing what you learned at the time rather than trying to 're-learn' the material from scratch.

Example Layout of the Outline Note-Taking Method:

Subject: Title

Topic Header 1
- Key idea 1
  - Details relating to idea 1
  - Details relating to idea 1

Topic Header 2
- Key idea 2
  - Details relating to idea 2
  - Details relating to idea 2

Topic Header 3
- Key idea 3
  - Details relating to idea 3
  - Details relating to idea 3

The Cornell Method

The Cornell note-taking method (my personal favorite) was designed at Cornell University by Walter Pauk and serves as a fantastic educational aid. Although the Cornell method was first introduced in the 1940s, it has stood the test of time and is one of the most popular note-taking methods today. In this fast-paced world, we are expected to learn at lightning speed and are pushed be the best at everything which is why taking the time to upgrade your ability to learn and record information is so crucial.

Students of all ages can use this method to enhance their learning skills. Let's learn how this can be implemented in reality and use it to create better, in-depth, and more structured notes.

You start with a blank page and divide it into two columns and one row at the bottom of the page. The right-hand column will be greater in width than the left-hand. In the narrow left-hand column, you will write down important cues such as keywords or questions. You can also use this to note any reminders or comments regarding the topic you are studying.

In wider right-hand column, you write down the notes related to the cues in the left column. Here, is where you expand on the thoughts and ideas, include some bullet points and diagrams as well as full sentences.

In the row beneath the two columns, you summarize the topic being taught in your own words so that recalling it becomes easier. Depending on how you like to take notes, you can increase or decrease the space for each column or row. For instance, some people are better at writing down ideas in their own words. They can have the summary section take more space on the page.

This is again, an efficient way to take notes and reduces the amount of time you have to spend reviewing and editing later. The reason for this is the summary section encourages you to speak your mind and explain things in your own words. Something that your mind concocts is easier to remember.

Example Layout of the Cornell Note-Taking Method:

Cues:	Notes:
Keywords	Expanded thoughts & ideas
Questions	Diagrams
Summary:	

Download your printable Cornell Method note paper from:
bit.ly/howtolearnfasterbook

Mind Mapping

Mind mapping is practically the polar opposite of linear note-taking. It is ideal to use during lectures, in a meeting, during a presentation or even when brainstorming ideas.

This method has the most visual layout from the four methods that we will be discussing in this book. Key thoughts, ideas and questions are spread out as subheadings around a main central heading/topic, where they are linked together (outwardly from the central heading) via labeled and unlabeled branches.

From this point you expand each subheading/subtopic further, linking your expanded thoughts and ideas in the same way. These connecting branches represent how your ideas connect as well as the direction of your train of thought at the time, which will make it feel easy to pick back up when you review and study from your mind map in the future. Repeat the process of expanding and linking ideas until your visual information map has taken shape.

This is a relatively simple but effective method of recording ideas and mapping out your thought process at the time of learning. Mind maps offer a great and easy to follow overview of the topic that was being discussed and its visual nature helps to promote recall when reviewed.

I often recommend that people combine the use of mind mapping with other note-taking techniques (such as the Cornell Method). For example, you can include a simple mind map to the right-hand column of your Cornell notes or reverse engineer your mind map later, by expanding it into either fully written Cornell or outline notes. By combining these methods together as described, your understanding and retention of the information in the mind mapped topic will be greatly supported.

As we discussed before, visuals are always a big help to improving your recall as well as aiding your ability to memorize information. By adding some bold colors, drawn images, and by associating icons with each subtopic your mind map will become more visually stimulating, and let's face it, more fun to revise from.

Example Layout of a Mind Map:

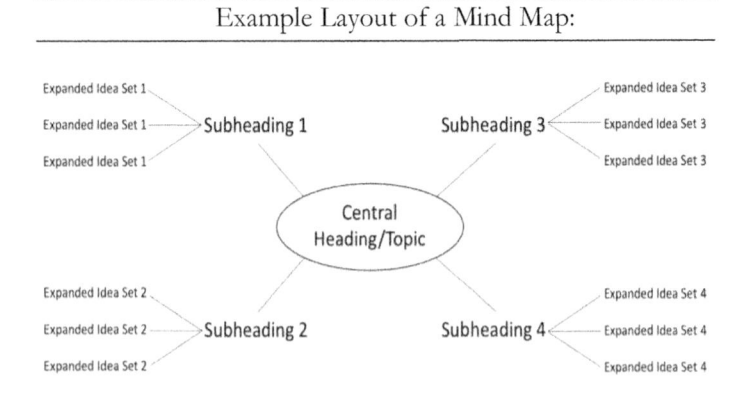

```
Expanded Idea Set 1                                    Expanded Idea Set 3
Expanded Idea Set 1 ──▶ Subheading 1     Subheading 3 ◀── Expanded Idea Set 3
Expanded Idea Set 1                                    Expanded Idea Set 3
                        ╲         ╱
                       ( Central   )
                       ( Heading/Topic )
                        ╱         ╲
Expanded Idea Set 2                                    Expanded Idea Set 4
Expanded Idea Set 2 ──▶ Subheading 2     Subheading 4 ◀── Expanded Idea Set 4
Expanded Idea Set 2                                    Expanded Idea Set 4
```

Bullet Journaling

Journaling has always been a fantastic way of recording thoughts and ideas as well as managing tasks. As mentioned earlier in the book, many super successful people keep a handwritten journal to help them plan, process and track their daily, weekly and monthly ideas as well as to schedule their future steps in a quick, clear and easy to follow manner. The bullet journaling technique helps you to track and manage your study plan and materials in a similar way, allowing you to curate your thoughts in a tangible, sleek manner.

The technique was designed by Ryder Carroll in the 1990s, so it's fairly modern in comparison to the other three methods that we have discussed in this chapter. Ryder had trouble keeping effective notes in school and wanted to come up with a simple and structured way that he could record information, track any deadlines, and easily revise from when needed to. It is a combination of different methods compiled into one single system.

Since I want you to grasp the basics here, we will start with the daily log method. Once mastered, you can make it more in depth and elaborative. It's worth mentioning here that as well as taking your subject notes, you can also add multiple tasks and routines into the mix as well.

To get started, you will need a regular notepad or diary. Designate the first couple of pages for indexing. A bullet journal's index pages work in the same way as a contents page of a book. It is used as a reference key so you can quickly skip to specific topic sections of your notes when you need to. Add to the index as you build your bullet journal note book up. You can use colored tabs, page numbers, headings, or all of these as index reference features. Whichever you feel works best for you.

In essence, the logs in a bullet journal are spaces where you can download task information from your brain onto a page in a simply structured manner. When taking specific subject notes, assign bullets for tasks, and dashes for task notes. It is best to keep your notes brief and clean. Try to stick to simple four to five-word sentences and key words, phrases and dates.

If there are additional notes or subtasks, you can use indented bullets under the original listed task. These subtasks can include key parts of the method that you are going to use to complete the assignment. For instance, if on a particular date, you want to complete a project outline and then on the following day, your goal is to have the project's introduction written, you can create two indented statements as the beginnings of a basic structured plan.

Now, as you begin to work on the tasks, you can check off each part of the listed plan with an X over the bullet.

You can also strike out the subtasks as you go. E.g. If you have completed the introduction, you can strike it off the list.

To keep any important details such as key research material suggestions and project deadline dates as visual as possible, you can circle or color code the related bullet point so that it can be found quickly.

To highlight the most important project tasks, you can add an asterisk after each subtask or before the bullet point. You can also choose to add an exclamation mark to make it pop from the page more.

At the end of each day, you go back and review the daily log tasks. Your goal here is to have the full list of accomplished daily tasks and the following day's log already prepared or at least taking shape.

This applies to note-taking as well. You can use a new page for each lecture and divide the topics accordingly. If there are any important points you wish to mark for later, you can add an asterisk or exclamation mark to it. As you continue to take notes in your journal, remember to keep adding to the index page at the front of the notepad.

You can also create monthly and future logs where you track all your goals, events and deadlines in the coming month and beyond. Try to keep it as simple as possible. One of the beauties of keeping a bullet journal is that the method should feel individually suited to you. There's no reason that you can't combine elements of this method with other methods discussed in this chapter. This will make your bullet journal totally personalized.

Summary

- The Outline Method – Highly structured and logical note-taking method

- The Cornell Method – Each page is structured into cues, notes and a summary.

- Mind Mapping – A visual note taking technique clearly showing links between ideas.

- Bullet Journaling – Create a personalized, well indexed set of notes including daily logs and check lists.

- Upgrading your note-taking ability isn't about always sticking rigidly to just one method. Combine the suggested techniques in a way that best suits you to get the most out of them.

Chapter 7
Supercharge Your Mental Focus

Your level of concentration plays a crucial role whether you are studying in class, working in an office, or reading a book. You have to have steady attention to accomplish those tasks efficiently. Concentration is defined as the mental process of focusing your mind on something particular, without distraction for a period of time. It could be a thought, an idea, or a task. Our brain, in many ways, is like a computer. We receive information, process it, compute it and then output it in some way.

Many people have a hard time truly focusing their minds. Our levels of concentration aren't always ideal. On some days, we may experience slower-than-normal response where nothing seems to be going the way we want it to. This can lead to immense frustration. You probably have had those instances where after reading a whole section from a book, you have no idea what it was about. As my mother used to say, sometimes it feels as though it has gone in through the eyes and out of the ears! At another time, you could read the same section of the book, and it feels like the easiest piece of information in the world, and you start to wonder why it didn't go in the first time.

Not only does poor concentration and inability to focus hinder performance, but it also leads to a huge loss of our most valuable asset... Time. Something that can be accomplished in one hour ends up taking several. This is a prime demotivator and is the enemy of efficiency and productivity.

An unfocused mind is a wandering mind. It's virtually impossible to have fully fixed concentration for one hundred percent of the time. Even when we are in the middle of an important task, our minds can stray twenty to forty percent (Mautz, May 2019). Keeping our attention fixated voluntarily takes a huge amount of effort. Luckily, there are many ways we can build up our mental stamina to prevent the mind from wandering to the same degree and instead hold a much stronger focus but, before we get to that, let's explore how the brain builds focus in the first place, how we can hear someone's conversation from the middle of the room, focus on the people in the other car while driving, or finish several chores at once. How does the mind build concentration when it is entertaining several other thoughts at the same time?

How the Brain Builds Focus

Remember, in chapter 2, we talked about system 1 (unconscious thought processes) and system 2 (conscious thought processes)? Both of these are responsible for controlling our attention. System 1 controls our involuntary and automatic decisions and is always on. It's the link in our brain that processes the stimuli received from the environment. We use this to turn our heads when we hear someone call our name. It is also responsible for causing us a to have a 'mini heart attack' when we see a spider crawl across the wall.

System 2 is involved in running the voluntary parts of the brain. System 2 processes the suggestions placed by system 1 and finalizes decisions. It also decides where we should allocate our attention. The surprising thing about these systems is that we assume that most of the decisions we take are conscious aka decisions made by system 2. However, this isn't true. System 1 is what feeds suggestions into the brain most of the time, which means that even though we believe that we base our decisions entirely on our conscious thought process, they are usually influenced by and therefore a product of our automatic thinking.

Although the second system mostly runs our focus and concentration, there is only so much that it can do. There are continuous innumerable distractions that the brain has to fight against which can make it difficult to stay focused.

Building on that, it is also important to note that there is no attention center in the brain. Our ability to focus and concentrate on something relies on a widespread network of brain regions that collectively work together to create the attentional system. This system closely interfaces with your actions, feelings, and thoughts and helps them operate more efficiently.

Therefore, if we can become capable of engaging this network on demand, over time we can improve our focus as well as build our focus's stamina.

The attentional system accesses most regions in every lobe of the brain. At the time that information is received by the brain, the region linked to that information is activated to allow for the specific attention that is required, for example visual or auditory information. Once the new information has been received, the related region of the brain directs your attention to where it needs to be. For example, some tasks require conscious attention and a lot of focus, like addressing a math problem. Others require hardly any effort to process at all and are almost automatic with little conscious attention, like the way that you brush your teeth.

Distractions, Distractions, Distractions...

Distractions come in different shapes and sizes. Some are big enough to take away all your attention at once, while the smaller ones target you differently. The good news is that how you react to these distractions can be tamed, and we'll investigate how later in the chapter. Before that, we should try to understand why we react to distractions in the way that we do. Let's review how Daniel Goleman describes distractions in his book *Focus: The Hidden Driver of Excellence*. According to him, distractions can either be sensory or emotional. Sensory distractions are comprised of all the things that are around you. Emotional distractions are comprised of your internal dialogue, thought process, and other important events happening in the present.

For example, if you are in an emotional state of mind and something is bothering you, you will be more than likely to have a difficult time concentrating on anything else. Goleman believes that this is because if something weighs heavy on the mind to the point of distraction, your brain prioritizes all focus on trying to find a solution for it, and until it can, your mind won't feel at rest.

These emotional worries and distractions plague us the most. Of course, you can try to block them out and force yourself to focus on something else, but you are likely to keep repeatedly drifting back and forth to the issue. When we keep ping-ponging from one topic to another, mental energy gets depleted making it harder to think, comprehend, memorize, and recall.

Think back to the example discussed earlier, and what is likely to happen if we try to just block out the inner critic's negative dialogue. How it doesn't go away but instead seems to grow louder. Attempting to block out worrisome distractions works out in a similar way, because by simply trying to block it out, the mind becomes fatigued, then distracted, then unproductive. In short, this will end up making us lose sight of our goals and what we must do to achieve them.

Distractions can end up being costly. They eat up our time and lead to forgetfulness, which means more rushed work with more mistakes, poor focus, and low productivity.

Being unable to focus well continuously chips away at everything we do or want to do which can affect self-confidence and can lead to us abandoning our plans and giving up on our goals.

So, what can be done about such distractions?

Beating Study Distractions to Build Attention and Concentration

As mentioned above, taming distractions is possible. There are several effective ways to keep you focused, productive and moving towards what you want, but in my experience the absolute best technique is to set or reviewing your goals (as discussed in chapter 1).

You don't always have to juggle between work, a side project, report, or assignment simultaneously. You can always break it down into smaller, more believable, and achievable task sets. There is such motivational power in both writing and reviewing the exact things that you want to achieve alongside the planned methods that you'll use to achieve them.

We have already talked about the hugely positive effects setting daily and weekly goals can have. We have also learned how to start with a time frame and a plan. Use this knowledge to your advantage and start setting your goals, making your plans and giving them realistic but unmovable time frames for when you will accomplish them. I always recommend that your weekly and daily goals are reviewed and scored every day. The point of reviewing these daily is so that you can adjust them as needed to keep motivated. It's not about just making it easier. It's about finding the right balance to keep you motivated and on track. This is how to challenge yourself and achieve things that you never thought you could.

If you are working on your laptop, set timers that are visible so that you remain alert and leave no room for any wandering thoughts in the mind. Also, set your phone aside. People are addicted to their mobile devices. It's gotten to the point that some people imagine feeling their phone vibrate in their pocket even when it isn't in there! As mentioned earlier, unless you are willing to unshackle yourself from your cell phone while you work, it will remain one of your biggest distractions. Of course, be sensible about it, I'm not suggesting that you go crazy. For example, if you are waiting on an important call, just set it to vibrate only, and place it face down on your desk just out of your working visual scope.

Alongside removing your phone from the equation, I suggest that if you're working on your laptop or desktop, switch off your social media notifications. If you don't, you'll find that whenever one pops up on screen, it is almost impossible to resist clicking on it. And let's face it, seeing what your friend had for their lunch today or the latest video clip of a cat being startled by a cucumber etc. can wait!

Everybody's different and as discussed earlier, everybody learns information slightly differently. Sometimes to positively change your state of mind, you simply have to change the physical environment that you're in. Allow me to give you a couple of examples.

Some individuals find that they work best in a space with some hustle and bustle going on in the background. Working in this kind of atmosphere helps them to 'zone out' and enter a state of productive focus. It's not uncommon for an individual to grab their laptop and head to a coffee shop in town. Once there it's almost as if they are able to change their mental state into a 'work mode' of sorts.

On the other hand, some individuals (I include myself in this bracket) can only reach a true state of productive focus when there is absolute pin-drop silence in the background. With the exception of the library, it's not always possible to find a totally quiet place to study or work, so what then? Personally, I find that by wearing my headphones (switched off) blocks out enough residual sound that I can enter a focused 'work mode' almost anywhere.

What would you say is your preference? Are you the kind of person that works best when there is some background noise or total silence? If you find that you are regularly procrastinating when you should be focusing, perhaps it's time to try switching up your environment to see if you can change your mental state to your own 'work mode'.

If you feel that a lack of motivation is the reason your focus wanes, then try setting yourself some small rewards for every successful study or work chunk completed. Rewards go a long way to encourage you to keep moving. You can set both immediate and gradual rewards. A reward doesn't have to be extravagant. It can be something that is a simple celebration of your hard work.

Some great examples of this are, checking off something you have completed from your daily goals sheet or bullet journal, or writing your daily score as a 10 out of 10 at the end of the day. These simple suggestions give a brilliant sense of achievement and give you the same feeling that you would get from a small win. Consistently awarding yourself these small wins is a brilliant way to keep your motivation pumping. Remember to celebrate your successes along the way and use your inner motivator to reinforce what you're doing with some internal positive (and truthful) language.

If you recall, in chapter 5: *The 7 Steps to Faster Learning*, we talked about creating a learning schedule. How the simple keys to a productive study or work session goes hand in hand with having a quality plan of action. Here's a brief reminder of the main points discussed earlier. Forget about the 'scatter gun' approach! Before you start your 50 minute timer, make sure that you know the topic that you're going to be focusing on. To make the most of your scheduled time, ensure that you have all the required material to hand before you start. Declutter your workspace (#fengshui) and move all distractions out of your eye line (where possible) apart from what you need for your next scheduled study time chunk. Remind yourself what you want to get out of your study or work session, start the timer and get to it. Being organized with a decent plan beforehand is the equivalent to using a road map to success. It prevents detours, time wastage, and gets you to exactly where you want to be.

Why Should You Take Short Breaks?

Our attention spans are rather short. Some research suggests that humans have a fleeting attention span of as little as eight or less seconds (Bosse et al., 2007). This stat feels a bit like a smack in the face for those of us who are on a journey of self-improvement doesn't it? As technology advances our attention spans seem to reduce. We are constantly seeking out an app or some sort of life hack for everything we do in an attempt to remove the usual necessary hard work that is required to fulfil a task. It's almost as if we have forgotten how to focus, research and remember, and let's face it, why would our brains even try to remember anything when all we have to do is click a button on our mobile device and ask Google?

No wonder we have such a hard time being productive and staying focused today! Now don't get me wrong, I'm not trying to devalue technology in any way. Technological advancements are an incredible thing, they are helping us to continuously move mankind forwards. I'm just attempting to point out that more often than not, we end up rushing to these technologies rather than learning a skill fully, truly understanding the information we're researching, or exercising our brain's memory and recall. This can lead to us sometimes feeling at a loss when we do sit down to do something. When feeling this way our state of mind is affected, our focus diminishes and the only thing that we can think about is taking a break!

We've already spent quite a bit of time earlier, discussing methods to drastically improve mental focus, long term memory and the ability to accurately recall detailed information. We've talked about the importance of working in predetermined time chunks to make sure that your productivity remains high. You may be thinking 'but surely, to be more productive, shouldn't I just work for 5 or 6 hours straight with no breaks?'. If this valid thought crossed your mind, I wouldn't blame you. But try to remember that we are looking at the output volume of quality of work, rather than the number of non-stop hours worked. The rewards for your labor are found in the goals you have hit and from the work that you have produced to a high standard. Unfortunately, there are no medals awarded for how long it has taken you. What do I mean by this?

Taking breaks is a good thing. Of course, they shouldn't be the only thing that's keeping you motivated but factually, they are an important part of producing high quality work. It is believed by productivity experts that when we enter a focused state to work on a task, we can maintain it for around a 50-90 minutes bracket. The findings are based on the ultradian rhythms that last for 90 minutes (Baer, 2013). After that, we start to lose focus as well as interest and thus, our brains demand a desperate break. In an article in *The Atlantic*, experts propose that stretches of 90 minutes can be hard to achieve. It has been seen that we reach our perfect productivity at 52 minutes and then take a short break of 17 minutes (Thompson, 2014).

This simply means that, to mindfully hold our highest levels of productivity, alertness, attentiveness, and focus, it is important that we find a correct rhythm to set our work and break times to which works for us as individuals.

One of the most common questions that many clients ask me when I suggest for them to study/work in time chunks with scheduled breaks to help boost their productivity is: what should I do during the break time?

There are so many suggestions that the list could be endless! In short, the idea here is to step away from what you were doing. The whole idea of taking a recess from work is to engage in something else for a short amount of time. However, people often think of this as an opportunity to catch up on emails or spend time on some other kind of research so that the next working session can be crunched down. Smart, but not really. The brain needs something fresh to ponder over, rather than going over the same sort of thing again.

A better suggestion to make the most of your liberated time is by doing something that feels rewarding, relatively easy, and mental stress-reducing. Basically, something that fits into your schedules break time, helps you to rekindle your motivation and that is suitable to your working environment.

In my opinion, the absolute best suggestion that I can give you here is to simply get up and get yourself moving!

Your body was designed to move. It craves mobility. Giving your arms and legs some room to stretch and move is an excellent way to utilize your break time. Maybe go for a short jog. If that doesn't work for you, perhaps take a brisk stroll, even up and down the stairs if that's your only option. If a stroll isn't an option, maybe walk over to the water fountain and have a quick chat with a fellow student/colleague while you're there. If none of these suggestions suit you it's not a problem, just get yourself in motion in any safe way that works for you.

Moderate levels of physical activity have been proven to release more of the neurotransmitters otherwise known as the 'happy hormones' dopamine (proven to help boost memory, focus, mood and motivation) and serotonin (proven to help improve calmness, focus, learning and happiness) into the brain, along with a medley of 'feel-good' endorphins. By exposing yourself to increased levels of these hormones during your scheduled break is almost like giving your mind a chance to 'reboot' meaning that you are more likely to return to your desk with greater vigor, more motivation, and a focused happy brain.

It's time to stop over thinking. How is that even possible, you might wonder? Here's an example of what I mean that I'm sure you'll be familiar with. Imagine that you're trying to focus with all your might, to find the solution to a problem, but no matter how hard you try, the answer just doesn't seem to come. Then you give your brain the chance to mentally 'reboot' during a break (get up and move your body) and during that time you manage to stop thinking about the problem for a few moments. Then as if by magic, the solution just seems to pop into your head without any effort at all.

But why does this happen? Remember earlier when we discussed how memory works and the duel-process theory? This is a prime example of how automatic thought (system 1) comes into play. Once we have allowed the problem to move into the unconscious part of the mind it gets to work without the conscious analytical part interfering.

Whether you want to excel at a sport, achieve top grades in college, master a new skill, or improve on an existing one, training your mental focus is imperative. Having a laser like focus on the goals you want to achieve, and then actively applying yourself to train your brain to consistently use the strategies, means, ideas, and resources that help you to keep moving towards your goals in my opinion shows powerful and dedicated mental focus.

You must continuously polish your skillsets, put your mind to work, eliminate distractions and look after your physical and mental health in order to build the habits needed to keep expanding your knowledge. You can train your mind to think sharper, produce faster, and work in a more productive way. You can control any thought that arises, build upon the ideas that you have created, and find the means to bring those ideas into reality, if you are willing to apply yourself and learn how to supercharge your mental focus.

Summary

▸▸ Quality work is what counts, not the length of time you have spent producing it.

▸▸ Cut out the distractions and focus on what you're doing!

▸▸ Reward yourself for your hard work along the way to keep you motivated.

▸▸ Your physical work environment matters. Some people like hustle and bustle, and others need peace and quiet. Adapt the environment to suit your most productive 'work mode'.

▸▸ The body was designed to move. Move your body during your scheduled breaks to help boost your brain's 'happy hormones'.

▸▸ Stop overthinking! Allow your unconscious mind to look for solutions.

Download your daily score sheet and reference notes from:
bit.ly/howtolearnfasterbook

Chapter 8
The Power of Consistent Action

You might have heard the famous phrase that knowledge is power. We believe that the more information we consume, the greater our chances of success in all our endeavors. But how can we be sure that this abundance of knowledge makes us better off than when we didn't have it? Today, thanks to the internet, we all have access to pretty much every piece information and its accompanying research in existence, and all of this at the touch of a button or the swipe of a smart phone screen, true? Then, if knowledge is power, why do only some of us enjoy success? Why is there such a big gap between the people who have 'made it' and those who are struggling to find their way towards their goals? It has to be something more powerful than having access to vast amounts of information online or storing it in your head. Let me tell you what it is.

Knowledge on its own is not power because if it is not utilized in the way that it should be it is useless. Ask yourself this, do you remember all that you learned in school? Can you recall the trigonometry formulas or all the elements of the periodic table? What is the point of having learned a hundred skills but never using them? Does it not seem like a waste of time?

Knowledge is potential power. The knowing of something is only the first essential stepping-stone to success. Applied knowledge is true power. It's in the daily and weekly actions you take in the pursuit of your goals. It's in the ability to learn fast, improve your memory, and then applying the knowledge/skills —both new and old— like a boss that moves you forward towards your goals. It is found in the actions and activities you take in practice and in reality, time and time again, without distraction and without giving up. That is the simple truth of where your true power will come to light.

There is a possibility that those who are highly successful are 'naturally intelligent', persistent, more ambitious, and perhaps just lucky to have gotten this far. Being wise, ambitious, and persistent does help in taking you closer to your goals, but these abilities aren't things that you are born with, they are things that have been developed and they still aren't the defining factor. You may be super intelligent but have no idea how or where to channel it so what advantage does that really give you? You may have the patience and persistence to overcome any shortcomings but don't recognize what they are, if this is the case, how can you improve? Similarly, you may have plenty of ambition but not the right means to go with it, how is that any better than having no ambition? You may have been insanely lucky in all your pursuits, but you still need something more than luck to build and retain a successful life.

Consistent action is the key. If you focus on learning the skills that will move you towards your goals, you strengthen them daily and work on them until they are second nature, then you will almost certainly succeed in any pursuit. I think that this idea was best summed up by the legendary Bruce Lee, in one of his most memorable quotes.

"I fear not the man who has practiced 10,000 kicks once, but I fear the man who practiced one kick 10,000 times."

The one key ingredient that makes almost anything possible is, applied consistent action. Consistency can be defined as unflinching dedicated action towards a goal, ambition, or idea. If the goal, ambition, or idea is strong enough it will keep you fully engaged until it is seen through. Being consistent means that you won't indulge in pointless distractions while you're on the path. Being consistent means that you are fully aware of where you want to be and what you need to do to get there (this is potential power) and then following that up with the actions necessary to make it happen (this is true power).

To become consistent, we must commit to a continuous and sustained effort of action. This is a long-term commitment. This means that you have to stay true to your word, stick to the plan, and follow up on the tasks and exercises that must be done until your objectives are achieved. The foundations of consistency are built upon your ability to be take responsibility for what you want, and be accountable for your actions, choices, and decisions.

When you have taken enough repeated action, the formation of empowering habits that make accomplishing and retaining your goals easier are developed. These are the same habits that once developed make people say things to you like 'you're so lucky that it comes naturally to you', but as Samuel Goldwyn once put so aptly "The harder I work, the luckier I get".

Healthy habits keep you working at your optimal, giving your best, and setting better priorities. You remain focused and determined to keep going because you feel like you have all the resources at your aid. Healthy habits involve a good diet, quality sleep, and a moderate level of physical exercise to keep your body in shape and your mind switched on.

At the end of the day, you have to realize that before you can achieve great things, you must let go of any complaints and excuses. I haven't got the time; everyone has the same amount of time whether they are high achievers or low achievers. I'm too tired; stop watching late night TV and get to bed earlier. I don't know how to do it; then get online and learn how to do it. I'm not that lucky; get to work and you'll make your own luck. To be consistent, you must be responsible, be accountable, and take control of your actions and habits.

Being consistent also involves focusing on the present moment as you work, whilst maintaining a long-term view of the end goals overall. This allows you to track and review your progress in real-time and see how the compounding results impact your actions.

Some days it will seem that you keep coming face to face with obstacles which send you heading off down the wrong path. It can feel hard to push past these setbacks or to recorrect after a wrong turn, but you must hold strong and believe in your ability to achieve, to keep yourself motivated and moving forward. Accepting that mistakes are going to happen and are a only bad thing if you ignore or keep repeating them. As we discussed in chapter 3: *Fall down seven times, get up eight*, overcoming the fear of failure makes you open to acknowledging and learning from your mistakes.

Trying, failing, improving, and repeating is one of the ways that we refine and improve our skills.

Consistency plays a key role in self-improvement. Unbroken effort over time is how to build your skill set. Your work ethic towards what you want to achieve is powered by the reasoning behind why you want to achieve it.

Being consistent in your effort is a crucial element to succeeding in your endeavors. It leads to building strong mental patterns affecting what you think and how you feel. The habits created from the same effort, forms the subconscious actions that we take every day and that shape our futures. Your actions will lead you to where you deserve to be. We become what we consistently do.

Repeating something that moves you towards your target, enough times that it becomes a natural part of you and forms an automatic habit should be the aim. Consistent action is what enables you to reach high levels of achievement. This, in essence, is what differentiates success from failure, high achiever from low achiever, where you begin from where you end up, in any given field of endeavor.

Why Can't I Be Consistent in My Efforts?

Although the idea of being consistent is rather simple, many people still struggle with it. They start out motivated only to find themselves giving up. One reason, discussed earlier, is the number of distractions they are exposed to unknowingly. Being consistent requires discipline, commitment, and an unbending focus.

Apart from distractions, another reason that people lose their way and give up on their goals is that they don't understand the concept of delayed gratification. They want results fast. They want to become millionaires overnight, master a new language in a couple of days or hit their fitness goal in a week. Not only is that impractical, but it is also almost impossible. When you set long-term goals, you won't necessarily be receiving immediate grand results or five-star feedback, and you have to be okay with that. Don't lose hope and give up just because there isn't an obvious huge progression immediately. To be consistent you must free yourself from thoughts of instant gratification. One has to wait out, be patient, and continue to work with the same passion and determination to earn those rewards. You will make incremental improvements that will compound over time, and the results will be all the sweeter.

If you don't think this is the case, think about one of your skills that you are proud of. Perhaps, you are an excellent guitarist, a ballet dancer, are multilingual, or a master at what you do. Did you learn those skills in a day? Did you not practice playing the guitar every day for as long as you could until you were able to play effortlessly? Did you not practice dancing ever since you were little, and even if you twisted your ankles, you kept going until you were standing on your toes with grace? Did you not have to carry a pocket dictionary around, listen to audio CDs, watch movies with subtitles, and take classes when you were learning a new language until you became fluent?

Let's take it back even further. When a child is born, can it walk immediately? Of course not, it takes a child roughly 9 to 18 months on average to build up enough strength and coordination. Once the child is ready, it will usually stagger around the furniture gripping to it with all its might until confidence tells them to go for it. Then the child takes a step and falls. Gets up, tries again, takes two steps and falls again. Gets back up and keeps trying over and over until the child can do it without a second thought. Its pure unwavering determination has paid off and the child has achieved its goal.

No matter how average, good, or accomplished you are at what you do, it all took a serious amount of consistent actions to be who you are today. You might get praised for how well you play an instrument now, but you know how much work you have to put in to get there. You became accomplished because you applied yourself consistently towards learning and mastering it and followed a pattern of daily goals which focused you to get a little better each day.

Another reason you may struggle with consistency is that you are more focused on the end goal rather than the process. Remember I mentioned earlier that many successful people recognize that the journey to achievement requires far more attention than the destination of it. They know that if they plan their journey and dedicate themselves with unwavering focus, then the results of the destination are not just deserved but pretty much guaranteed. If you become fixated on the outcome alone, chances are it will work against you. How so? It is because any outcome that promises excellence and excitement requires a ton of patience, sacrifice and hard work over a period of time. If we can't commit ourselves to that, we can't expect to be rewarded.

Then, there is always aiming for perfection in everything. Aiming for perfection can harm your goal's progression. Instead, aim for daily improvement. Perfection is damn near impossible to achieve, therefore no matter how well you have done that day, how much you have achieved or how much closer you are to your goal, you will feel like you have fallen short. If you aim for perfection, you give power to feelings of negativity making it difficult to celebrate your day's successes. Aiming for progression is a far better mindset to have because you can feel good about any step forwards you have made and that will help you to push further and ultimately move quicker towards your goals.

To keep yourself moving forwards it's worth noting that if you are finding it difficult to consistently hit all of your daily goals, rather than beat yourself up about it, see it as an indication that you should consider adjusting them for now, so that they are attainable.

Conversely, if you are smashing all of your daily goals consistently, then it's time to push yourself a little further. Once your daily goals are second nature and have become some of your new productive habits, add some more daily goals to the list, then simply repeat the process and watch your productivity grow.

Another reason for inconsistent actions and limited results is a poor work ethic. Having a poor work ethic means purposely giving in to distractions, leaving things for the eleventh hour before performing a rush job, not following a plan of action, giving minimal effort, and saying to yourself 'that'll do'. Having a strong work ethic is demonstrated by the continuous, planned, and focused efforts and actions an individual makes to complete the tasks that will improve their knowledge and the skills that they need to keep moving forwards toward what they are striving for.

It's easy to get confused about what having a strong work ethic means. Some people believe that flogging themselves hard for an unplanned 16 hour day, distracted by all the minutiae that will ultimately lead nowhere, deserves some sort of fanfare. This of course is absolute nonsense, as an unplanned day equals an unproductive day, no matter how many hours you put in. Think of it as someone looking for gold in a coal mine. After a long day of back breaking hard work, they will have nothing to show for it.

People crave to look and feel busy. Generally speaking, people believe that busyness equals hard work, and hard work equals importance, and that in turn feeds their egos, 'cos let's face it, who doesn't like to feel important? The key point to remember here, is that results are what's important, not how busy you look or feel.

Thinly dispersing your efforts across a plethora of random things over a long period of time, in an attempt to look and feel busy is a waste of energy, lacks purpose, and as far as any tangible results goes, is unproductive. Instead, realize that by giving your undivided attention only to the tasks that move you forwards, will bare far greater fruit, in a much shorter amount of time. In other words, results are found in the quality of time put in and not necessarily in the quantity.

Does That Mean You Shouldn't Work Hard?

I am not against working long hours or working hard, and I'm certainly not attempting to belittle taking the time to give attention to relevant details.

I believe that if you have a goal and a clear plan, then you direct all of your energy towards completing the tasks and polishing the details on that plan, you will be productively working hard with a real focus and an actual purpose. Working in this way will help you to produce your most outstanding results in the shortest amount of time.

Example 1 – Having no plan: Imagine that you head to the gym without any idea of what you're going to work on once you get there, meaning that your workout is going to be unstructured to say the least. You do a bit of this and a bit of that, and only select exercises that you like, meaning that you end up wondering around the gym for almost 3 hours, then you head home. You repeat this pattern on and off for three months. I've seen this sort of thing time and time again, and trust me, you will never get the result you want this way!

Example 2 – Having a plan: Now change gear. You hit the gym with a structured program. You know what exercises you'll be doing, the order, the weights, the sets, the reps, and the rest periods. You don't particularly like some of the exercises on your program because of how hard you find them, but you get them done anyway because they're on your plan, and this plan is the map to your success. You're in and out of there in 1 hour and repeat this pattern for three months. Guess what? You get the results that you wanted.

Simple right?

In both of these examples, you have access to the exact same facility and equipment.

In example 1, even with access to everything that you technically need to achieve the results that you desire, working without a plan is hard and very time-consuming, it's also impossible to gauge how well you're doing, which is demotivating, and after all of your effort, results will be very limited.

Example 2 conversely shows that working with a plan is still hard work, but this time you know exactly what you have got to do which keeps you and all your energy focused, you can track your progress along the way which keeps you motivated, and once your plan is complete, you will reap first-class results. The only difference is that in example 2 you have a plan.

It's worth noting that creating an action-oriented work plan isn't about being totally ridged in your approach. Set your daily tasks in order starting with the most difficult tasks first. Getting these out of the way while your mind is fresh will make your life easier, and once they're completed, will help to keep you motivated. Set some realistic time frames for task completions to keep you focused. Allow some flex in your approach so you can adapt to what's in front of you without losing sight of the target.

Knowing why you are working towards something gives you a purpose. Having a purpose motivates you to stay focused and committed. The idea of having a compelling reason to act is a reinforcing factor that keeps pushing you forwards. It's constantly on your mind and brings a smile to your face because you can't stop visualizing success.

You don't have to work like a donkey all day, mindlessly plodding up and down with no clear idea where you're headed. You must focus on the goals that will help you improve and excel, not the ones that will take away your energy and leave you with nothing measurable in the end. Try to work smart by building the right habits. Set the right goals and track your progress as you go along. See if some of the steps can be sped up, adjusted, or removed, and whether original designs can be improved upon or not.

You will encounter some setbacks along the way. They happen to everyone. Try not to dwell on them as this can cripple your productivity. Instead acknowledge them, and then look at the bigger picture. Remind yourself of what you are aiming for and then adjust your plan to steer you back towards your target. When I encounter a setback, I try to think of it as merely a bump in the road that is still leading me toward success. This helps to keep me positive in my actions and confident of my abilities.

Remember that for every setback, there is always either a solution or an excuse.

You can be your best self and have things structured and good to go, thanks to short-term and long-term goals. Use them to stay on top of your game, boost productivity, and efficiency.

Summary

▸▸ Possessing knowledge is potential power. Applying knowledge is actual power.

▸▸ Continuous, unbroken effort over time compounds into outstanding results and an awesome skill set.

▸▸ Repetition builds habits, so make sure that you're repeating the right things!

▸▸ Always enjoy the journey. If you enjoy the process, you'll stick to the plan and your results will compound over time.

▸▸ Focus all your effort on what moves you forwards. Results are what's important, not how busy you look and feel.

▸▸ For every setback you will think of either a solution or an excuse.

Download your goal setting sheet and reference notes from:
bit.ly/howtolearnfasterbook

Conclusion

Not that long ago, the ability to memorize was considered a natural born skill. People, who could recall stories, talk about the myths and legends, review law, etc. remained the center of attention amongst all. However, since the advent of print media, their time and importance were short-lived. People were no longer reliant on someone's memory for the sharing valuable information. They had found a new way to look things up. Today, this job has been taken over by tech giants such as Google and Bing. Every piece of information is at our fingertips and available at the touch of a button and in the blink of an eye.

This might make you think, what's the point of memorizing anything when I can just review it online? True, but the art doesn't die with the artist, does it? The art of memorization is still a coveted skill that can move you towards achieving your desired goals. It can help you excel in your academics, further advance your career, hone your creative skills, and ultimately achieve your long-term goals.

Memorization is organizational discipline for the brain. Thanks to digitalization, our minds have become sloppy, lazy, and highly distracted. When was the last time you came up with a unique idea all on your own? When was the last time you forgot that idea a moment later and kicked yourself for it? Memorization helps build the brain's focus, is the reason that you can master new skills and it trains you to be industrious.

What about the times that you don't have access to the internet, like during an exam, in the classroom or in an interview? How will you look up material or accurately recall what you had tried to learn specifically for it, if you have a weak and haphazard memory? This will have a negative impact that could prevent you from reaching your true potential.

Let's briefly overview what we have discussed during our journey together.

Every amazing achievement starts with a goal. In the introductory chapter, we looked at how to set your most powerful goals, and how you can develop daily, weekly, and monthly plans of action to continuously push you towards them; we talked about how to drive your motivation so that you can achieve what you truly want in life. We talked about how you can use that new motivation to improve your memory, improve your ability to learn quickly and effectively, and to build laser like focus that will increase your productivity in both the short term and the long term.

In the following chapter, we discussed, how and why memories form, and the process of recall and memory retrieval in-depth. We also looked at of how you can effectively build them with methods ranging from the simple, how to remember a new acquaintance's name, to the advanced, walking around your memory palace like a modern-day Sherlock Holmes.

In the following chapter, we talked about the power of a winner's mindset and how failure should be viewed as a teacher rather than an enemy. We looked closely at some of the barriers thrown up by the fear of failure, and how they can stand in our way unless we're willing to cultivating a winner's mindset to battle against them with our internal dialogue.

In chapter 4, we discussed how limiting beliefs prevent us from fulfilling our dreams and how we can analyze, detect, and overcome them using self-reflection.

In chapter 5, we looked at how we can build memory, improve recall, and speed up the process of learning in seven simple steps. Each step challenged some of the traditional methods of learning and also improved on some classic, effective techniques. At the end of the chapter, briefly reviewed the inspirational John Kwik's FAST theory of how to learn anything at a rapid speed and improve recall.

In the following chapter, we elaborated on four brilliant note-taking methods: the outline, the Cornell, mind mapping, and bullet journaling. We talked about the benefits of each, and how you can use and combine them to your advantage. If you favor the Cornell method as I do, there are many good Cornell method notebooks available to purchase, I also have one available that can be found online.

In the final two chapters of the book, we focused on building attention and focus as well as discussing the power of committing yourself to take consistent action. We looked at the difficulties that some people encounter when trying to build their attention and stay consistent in their quest to achieve what they want. Later, we looked at some strategies to reinforce the ability to take consistent action as well as how we can build an unflinching focus.

If you have found the contents of this book useful and would like to increase the rate in which you learn and retain information further, you should consider reading my book *Learn Speed Reading – Fast* as your next skill building exercise.

I have been coaching for over two decades and have successfully helped thousands of people from all manner of backgrounds and abilities to overcome their fear of failure, master their ability to learn new skills quickly, enhance their focus, and achieve some of their most amazing and life changing goals.

Some of the ideas shared in this book aren't necessarily new. But I have recommended them because they have helped me to help so many people, which is why I am proud to now share them with you. I want you to become the best version of yourself, achieve your goals and win at life, whatever that might mean to you. If you want to get good grades, go get them. If you want to excel in your career, you can do it. If you want to set and achieve sky high goals, then get ready for lift off because if you have gotten this far then you have already shown a level of focus, action and commitment that can get you there.

One of the main messages in this book is how the power of consistent action is what makes your goals real. Focus on applying the knowledge you have learned in this book every day, because knowing and understanding something is just the first step. If you don't apply what you have learned, the knowledge is wasted – it's like having a blunt sword and the tools to sharpen it in your hands, but if you never use the tools, the sword will remain dull forever.

It is in the actual 'doing' that your greatness is unleashed. Your actions are what will build and strengthen your skill sets, and it's where every result that you desire can be found. Be focused on all your efforts, deliberate in your actions, diligent in your work, and celebrate your every success. That is what will lead you to glory.

If there is just one final thing that I could wish for readers to take away from this book, it is for them to realize the power that is hidden within their own self-belief. If you believe something is possible, then it is possible. If you believe that you can achieve your goals, then you will achieve them. If you truly believe in your passions, then they will become a prized part of your existence.

It's the belief you have in yourself that makes your dreams come to fruition. So go and build your abilities, learn, grow, and cultivate the mindset that you need to move you ever closer to your goals. I know that you have it in you to achieve all of these things.

All you have to do is believe.

Thanks for Reading

I just wanted to say thank you for taking the time to read through my book. I am truly grateful.

If you have found my book helpful, and if you have a few spare moments, I'd really appreciate you leaving me a review.

Please scan the appropriate QR code below with you cell phone camera or visit Amazon to leave a:

US Review   UK Review

Wishing you success in all your future endeavors.

Joseph Milano

- Joseph

Special thanks to my wife, my children, and my wonderful clients for all your encouragement to write this book and for your support during the process.

References

Alvernaz, A. (2020, June 18). *These limiting beliefs are preventing you from being successful.* Blog.trello.com. https://blog.trello.com/limiting-beliefs

Are your beliefs holding you back? (n.d.). Tonyrobbins.com. https://www.tonyrobbins.com/stories/unleash-the-power/are-your-beliefs-holding-you-back/

Aswell, S. (2019, January 8). *The 5-minute technique I use to defeat negative self-talk.* Healthline. https://www.healthline.com/health/mental-health/self-talk-exercises#How-to-use-the-5-minute-triple-column-technique-

Baer, D. (2013, June 19). *Why you need to unplug every 90 minutes.* Fast Company. https://www.fastcompany.com/3013188/why-you-need-to-unplug-every-90-minutes

Barile, N. (2017, June 28). *The perfect high school summer reading list to prevent brain drain.* Hey Teach! https://www.wgu.edu/heyteach/article/the-perfect-high-school-summer-reading-list-to-prevent-brain-drain1706.html

Barile, N. (2018, January 16). *Exercise and the brain: How fitness impacts learning.* Hey Teach! https://www.wgu.edu/heyteach/article/exercise-and-brain-how-fitness-impacts-learning1801.html#:~:text=Ratey%20writes%20that%20exercise%20improves

Becker, L. J. (1978). Joint effect of feedback and goal setting on performance: A field study of residential energy conservation. *Journal of Applied Psychology, 63*(4), 428–433. https://doi.org/10.1037/0021-9010.63.4.428

Benninger, M. (2019, May 31). *The psychology behind your fear of failure - blinkist magazine.* Www.blinkist.com. https://www.blinkist.com/magazine/posts/psychology-behind-fear-failure

Blackman, A. (2018, August 11). *What are self-limiting beliefs? +How to overcome them successfully.* Business Envato Tuts+. https://business.tutsplus.com/tutorials/what-are-self-limiting-beliefs--cms-31607

Bosse, M.-L., Tainturier, M. J., & Valdois, S. (2007). Developmental dyslexia: The visual attention span deficit hypothesis. *Cognition, 104*(2), 198–230. https://doi.org/10.1016/j.cognition.2006.05.009

Bounds, G. (2010, October 5). *How handwriting trains the brain.* The Wall Street Journal. https://www.wsj.com/articles/SB10001424052748704631504575531932754922518?utm_source=zapier.com&utm_medium=referral&utm_campaign=zapier&utm_source=zapier.com&utm_medium=referral&utm_campaign=zapier

Brandner, R. (2019, September 13). *Effective note taking in lectures and class using mind maps - focus*. Focus. https://www.mindmeister.com/blog/effective-note-taking/

Bygraves, M. (2019, July 19). *You should treat your brain like A muscle: Think exercise*. Peak. https://blog.peak.net/2019/07/19/is-your-brain-a-muscle/

Castrillon, C. (2019, July 9). *Why A growth mindset is essential for career success*. Forbes. https://www.forbes.com/sites/carolinecastrillon/2019/07/09/why-a-growth-mindset-is-essential-for-career-success/?sh=39768bca28b5

Challis, B. H., Velichkovsky, B. M., & Craik, F. I. M. (1996). *Levels-of-Processing effects on a variety of memory tasks: New findings and theoretical implications*. Consciousness and Cognition, *5*(1-2), 142–164. https://doi.org/10.1006/ccog.1996.0009

Chamberlain, R. (2018, January 28). *Brain power: Limiting life through limiting beliefs*. Unstuck Psychological. https://www.unstuckpsych.com/blog/brain/

Cherry, K. (2021, April 13). *How to deal with the fear of failure*. Verywell Mind. https://www.verywellmind.com/what-is-the-fear-of-failure-5176202

Cohen, N., Margulies, D. S., Ashkenazi, S., Schaefer, A., Taubert, M., Henik, A., Villringer, A., & Okon-Singer, H. (2016). *Using executive control training to suppress amygdala reactivity to aversive information*. NeuroImage, *125*, 1022–1031. https://doi.org/10.1016/j.neuroimage.2015.10.069

Cole, S., Balcetis, E., & Zhang, S. (2013). *Visual perception and regulatory conflict: Motivation and physiology influence distance perception.* Journal of Experimental Psychology: General, 142(1), 18–22. https://doi.org/10.1037/a0027882

Colvin, G. (2019). Talent is overrated : what really separates world-class performers from everyone else. Nicholas Brealey Publishing.

Compton, R. J. (2003). *The interface between emotion and attention: A review of evidence from psychology and neuroscience.* Behavioral and Cognitive Neuroscience Reviews, 2(2), 115–129. https://doi.org/10.1177/1534582303002002003

Cooper, B. B. (2014, February 8). *The brain science of controlling our attention & gaining focus.* Buffer Resources. https://buffer.com/resources/the-science-of-focus-and-how-to-improve-your-attention-span/

Cornell note taking —the best way to take notes explained. (2017, August 9). Medium; GoodNotes Blog. https://medium.goodnotes.com/study-with-ease-the-best-way-to-take-notes-2749a3e8297b

Empty your cup. (2021). C2.com. https://wiki.c2.com/?EmptyYourCup

Erin, S. (2017, May 17). *Your "why" matters: The 10 benefits of knowing your purpose in life.* Goalcast. https://www.goalcast.com/2017/05/17/10-benefits-of-knowing-your-purpose-in-life/

Fannin, J. L., & Williams, R. M. (2012). *Leading-Edge neuroscience reveals significant correlations between beliefs, the whole-brain state, and psychotherapy.* Innermost Sherpa; https://psych-k.com/wp-content/uploads/2013/10/FanninWilliams.CQ-copy.pdf

Goeke, N. (2015, September 7). *The study plan schedule strategy (that actually works!).* Develop Good Habits. https://www.developgoodhabits.com/study-schedule/#Final_Thoughts_on_the_Study_Schedule_That_Works

Greshko, M. (2019, March 4). *The human memory—facts and information.* Science. https://www.nationalgeographic.com/science/article/human-memory

Haden, J. (2018, December 13). *These 10 scientific ways to learn anything faster could change everything you know about dramatically improving your memory.* Inc.com. https://www.inc.com/jeff-haden/these-10-scientific-ways-to-learn-anything-faster-could-change-everything-you-know-about-dramatically-improving-your-memory.html

Houston, E. (2019, June 19). *What is goal setting and how to do it well.* PositivePsychology.com. https://positivepsychology.com/goal-setting/

How memory works. (n.d.). Bokcenter.harvard.edu. https://bokcenter.harvard.edu/how-memory-works#:~:text=Memory%20also%20gives%20individuals%20a

Improving memory - Harvard health. (2019). Harvard Health; Harvard Health. https://www.health.harvard.edu/topics/improving-memory

James, G. (2019, October 23). *What goal-setting does to your brain and why it's spectacularly effective.* Inc.com. https://www.inc.com/geoffrey-james/what-goal-setting-does-to-your-brain-why-its-spectacularly-effective.html

Jobes, D. (2007, October 30). *The best memory trick - visualization & association.* Memory-Improvement-Tips.com. https://www.memory-improvement-tips.com/best-memory-trick.html

Klauser, H. A. (2001). *Write it down make it happen: Knowing what you want and getting it.* Amazon (1st edition, pp. 1–256). Scribner. https://www.amazon.com/Write-Down-Make-Happen-Knowing-ebook/dp/B000FC0X1O

Klemm, W. R. (2013, January 12). *Five reasons that memory matters | psychology today.* Www.psychologytoday.com. https://www.psychologytoday.com/us/blog/memory-medic/201301/five-reasons-memory-matters#:~:text=The%20exercise%20of%20the%20memory

Koch, R. (2020, December 8). *Using the power of self-belief to create success.* Entrepreneur. https://www.entrepreneur.com/article/361019

Koort, K. (2014, November 20). *7 questions you must ask when setting goals.* Weekdone. https://blog.weekdone.com/team-goal-setting-questions-to-ask/

Korba, R. J. (1990). *The rate of inner speech*. Perceptual and Motor Skills, *71*(3), 1043–1052. https://doi.org/10.2466/pms.1990.71.3.1043

Lipton, B. H. (2016). The biology of belief : Unleashing the power of consciousness, matter & miracles. Hay House, Inc.

Locke, E. A. (1968). *Toward a theory of task motivation and incentives*. Organizational Behavior and Human Performance, *3*(2), 157–189. https://doi.org/10.1016/0030-5073(68)90004-4

Lucas, L. (n.d.). *Chapter 9: Memory and information processing | EDUC 1300: Effective learning strategies*. Courses.lumenlearning.com. https://courses.lumenlearning.com/austincc-learningframeworks/chapter/chapter-9-memory-and-information-processing/

MacLeod, A. K., Coates, E., & Hetherton, J. (2007). *Increasing well-being through teaching goal-setting and planning skills: Results of a brief intervention*. Journal of Happiness Studies, *9*(2), 185–196. https://doi.org/10.1007/s10902-007-9057-2

Man in the arena speech - theodore roosevelt 1910. (n.d.). Www.worldfuturefund.org. http://www.worldfuturefund.org/Documents/maninarena.htm

Mariama-Arthur, K. (2017, February 24). *Why mindset mastery is vital to your success*. Entrepreneur.

https://www.entrepreneur.com/article/285466#:~:text=Th e%20truth%20is%20that%20mindset

Maw, A. (2019, March 25). *6 strategies for setting weekly goals you'll actually meet*. The JotForm Blog. https://www.jotform.com/blog/setting-weekly-goals/

Mccarthy, E. (2015, April 23). *Roosevelt's "the man in the arena."* Mentalfloss.com. https://www.mentalfloss.com/article/63389/roosevelts-man-arena

McRoberts, S. (2017, November 20). *Me, myself and I: 4 ways to harness that nagging voice in your head*. Entrepreneur. https://www.entrepreneur.com/article/303456

Memory recall/retrieval | types, processes, improvement & problems. (2019, September 25). The Human Memory. https://human-memory.net/memory-recall-retrieval/

Metivier, A. (2013, September 22). *Magnetic memory method - memory improvement made easy with anthony metivier*. Magnetic Memory Method - How to Memorize with a Memory Palace. https://www.magneticmemorymethod.com/how-to-remember-things/

Mind mapping basics - simplemind. (2017). SimpleMind. https://simplemind.eu/how-to-mind-map/basics/

Mindvalley. (2017). *Speed learning: Learn in half the time | jim kwik*. YouTube. https://www.youtube.com/watch?v=0r1LTe5KkSA

Morisano, D., Hirsh, J. B., Peterson, J. B., Pihl, R. O., & Shore, B. M. (2010). *Setting, elaborating, and reflecting on personal goals improves academic performance.* Journal of Applied Psychology, *95*(2), 255–264. https://doi.org/10.1037/a0018478

Mueller, P. A., & Oppenheimer, D. M. (2014). *The pen is mightier than the keyboard.* Psychological Science, *25*(6), 1159–1168. https://doi.org/10.1177/0956797614524581

O'Neill, M. (2018, August 29). *What is the difference between goals and objectives: Examples of an actionable business planning process.* Www.samewave.com. https://www.samewave.com/posts/the-difference-between-goals-and-objectives-create-an-actionable-business-planning-process

Orr, R. (2010, October 30). *REVEALED: 8 goal setting questions to ask yourself.* Roborr.net. https://roborr.net/8-goal-setting-questions/

Outline notes: How to use this method for better note-taking. (2017, October 19). Medium; GoodNotes Blog. https://medium.goodnotes.com/how-the-outline-note-taking-method-works-f0808ea2cbfa

Ovsyannnykov, I. (2020, March 23). *5 reasons why mindset is essential for success.* Inspirationfeed. https://inspirationfeed.com/importance-of-mindset-for-personal-success/

Patel, N. (2014, December 11). *When, how, and how often to take a break*. Inc.com; Inc. https://www.inc.com/neil-patel/when-how-and-how-often-to-take-a-break.html

Paul Ramsden: We need to ensure quality of university teaching, not quantity. (2006, October 31). The Guardian. https://www.theguardian.com/education/2006/oct/31/universityteaching.highereducation3

Possing, S. (2020, July 24). *How to set daily goals*. WikiHow. https://www.wikihow.com/Set-Daily-Goals

Riopel, L. (2019, June 14). *The importance, benefits, and value of goal setting*. PositivePsychology.com. https://positivepsychology.com/benefits-goal-setting/

Robbins, T. (n.d.). *10 Steps to believe in yourself and achieve amazing results*. Tonyrobbins.com. https://www.tonyrobbins.com/building-confidence/how-to-believe-in-yourself/

Roxine Kee. (2019, January 29). *How the bullet journal can make you a more productive student*. College Info Geek. https://collegeinfogeek.com/bullet-journal/

Schaffner, A. K. (2020, October 15). *Living with your inner critic: 8 helpful worksheets and activities*. PositivePsychology.com. https://positivepsychology.com/inner-critic-worksheets/

Schunk, D. H. (1985). *Participation in goal setting: Effects on self-efficacy and skills of learning-disabled children*. The Journal of Special Education, *19*(3), 307–317. https://doi.org/10.1177/002246698501900307

Schwartzbard, J. (n.d.). *How focus works in your brain - better mind*. Bettermind. https://www.bettermind.com/articles/how-focus-works-in-your-brain/#:~:text=Your%20brain%20directs%20focus%20capability

Step 3: Memory retrieval | boundless psychology. (2019). Lumenlearning.com. https://courses.lumenlearning.com/boundless-psychology/chapter/step-3-memory-retrieval/

Stuifbergen, A. K., Becker, H., Timmerman, G. M., & Kullberg, V. (2003). The use of individualized goal setting to facilitate behavior change in women with multiple sclerosis. Journal of Neuroscience Nursing, 35(2), 94–99. https://doi.org/10.1097/01376517-200304000-00005

The 5 golden principles of goal setting | bookboon blog. (2012, May 4). Bookboon.com. https://bookboon.com/blog/2012/05/the-5-golden-principles-of-goal-setting/

The brain's ability to concentrate. (n.d.). UniversalClass.com. https://www.universalclass.com/articles/psychology/the-brain-ability-to-concentrate.htm

The critical inner voice explained. (2009, June 18). PsychAlive. https://www.psychalive.org/critical-inner-voice/

Thompson, D. (2014, September 17). *A formula for perfect productivity: Work for 52 minutes, break for 17*. The Atlantic.

https://www.theatlantic.com/business/archive/2014/09/science-tells-you-how-many-minutes-should-you-take-a-break-for-work-17/380369/

Tosi, H. L., Locke, E. A., & Latham, G. P. (1991). *A theory of goal setting and task performance*. The Academy of Management Review, *16*(2), 480. https://doi.org/10.2307/258875

Vincent, P. J., Boddana, P., & MacLeod, A. K. (2004). *Positive life goals and plans in parasuicide*. Clinical Psychology & Psychotherapy, *11*(2), 90–99. https://doi.org/10.1002/cpp.394

Visual imagery | classroom strategy. (2013, March 19). Reading Rockets. https://www.readingrockets.org/strategies/visual_imagery#:~:text=Good%20readers%20construct%20mental%20images

Vos, R. de. (2015, September 30). *The power of WHY: Why having a why is so important!* www.linkedin.com. https://www.linkedin.com/pulse/power-why-having-so-important-rosanne-de-vos#:~:text=Your%20why%20serves%20as%20a

Vozza, S. (2016, August 30). *Six brain hacks to learn anything faster*. Fast company; Fast Company. https://www.fastcompany.com/3063173/six-brain-hacks-to-learn-anything-faster

Weber, J. P. (2017, July 14). *The power of your internal dialogue*. Psychology Today. https://www.psychologytoday.com/us/blog/having-sex-wanting-intimacy/201707/the-power-your-internal-dialogue

West, B. (n.d.). *7 questions you need to ask yourself when setting goals – life as britny*. Life as Britny. Retrieved April 20, 2021, from https://lifeasbritny.com/questions-to-ask-yourself-when-setting-goals/#:~:text=Are%20you%20setting%20goals%20that

Wikipedia Contributors. (2019, April 18). *Mental image*. Wikipedia; Wikimedia Foundation. https://en.wikipedia.org/wiki/Mental_image

Williams, R. (2020, January 28). *How self-limiting beliefs can sabotage our success and happiness*. Medium. https://raybwilliams.medium.com/how-self-limiting-beliefs-can-sabotage-our-success-and-happiness-dc38f2aded08

Williams, S. R., & Fletcher, L. N. (2019). *A dendritic substrate for the cholinergic control of neocortical output neurons*. Neuron, 101(3), 486-499.e4. https://doi.org/10.1016/j.neuron.2018.11.035

Printed in Great Britain
by Amazon

12021719R00099